FLORIDA STATE
UNIVERSITY LIBRARIES

APR 9 1997

TALLAHASSEE, FLORIDA

May Swenson

A Poet's Life in Photos

I LOOK AT MY HAND

I look at my hand and see
it is also his and hers;
the pads of the fingers his,

the wrists and knuckles hers.
In the mirror my pugnacious eye
and ear of an elf, his;

my tamer mouth and slant
cheekbones hers.
His impulses my senses swarm,
her hesitations they gather.
Father and Mother
who dropped me,

an acorn in the wood,
repository of your shapes
and inner streams and circles,

you who lengthen toward heaven,
forgive me
that I do not throw

the replacing green
trunk when you are ash.
When you are ash, no
features shall there be,
tangled of you,
interlacing hands and faces

through me
who hide, still hard,
far down under your shades—

and break my root, and prune my buds,
that what can make no replica
may spring from me.

May Swenson

A Poet's Life in Photos

R.R. Knudson
Suzzanne Bigelow

with foreword by Richard Wilbur

UTAH STATE UNIVERSITY PRESS LOGAN, UTAH

PS
3537
W4786
Z727
1996

This project is made possible by a grant from the Utah Humanities Council.

Utah State University Press
Logan, Utah 84322-7800

Typography by WolfPack

Copyright © 1996 by The Literary Estate of May Swenson. All rights reserved.
Foreword copyright © 1990 by Richard Wilbur. All rights reserved. Mr. Wilbur's foreword was originally delivered as a memorial tribute at the American Academy and Institute of Arts and Letters Dinner Meeting, November 8, 1990.

No part of this book may be reproduced or transmitted in any form or by any means, electronic or mechanical, including photocopying, recording, or any information storage and retrieval system, without permission in writing from the Literary Estate of May Swenson.

Library of Congress Cataloging-in-Publication Data
Knudson, R. Rozanne, 1932–
May Swenson : a poet's life in photos / R.R. Knudson, Suzzanne Bigelow ; with a foreword by Richard Wilbur.
p. cm.
ISBN 0-87421-218-9
1. Swenson, May—Pictorial works. 2. Women poets, American—20th century—Biography—Pictorial works. I. Bigelow, Suzzanne, 1929– . II. Title.
PS3537.W4786Z727 1996
811'.54—dc20
[B] 96-35686
CIP

The poems "My Mother and Father Came to See," "Prison Architecture," and eleven lines from "The Desk. The Body" are published here for the first time. Several poems are collected here for the first time but were previously published as follows: in *Utah Sings*, "Creation"; in *Ploughshares*, "A Rescue"; in *Poetry*, "The Rest of My Life"; in *The Yale Review*, "Sleeping with Boa."

Other poems were previously published as indicated on page 167, which constitutes an extension of this copyright page.

Contents

Frontispoem: I Look at My Hand ii
Foreword by Richard Wilbur 1

1 To Utah! 8
2 Love at Home 21
3 New York, New York 38
4 In the Village 54
5 A Purdue Interlude 84
6 Sea Cliff, Long Island 92
7 Home to Utah 114
8 Afterwords / Afterphotos 128

Anthology: A Life in Poems 133

The Truth Is Forced 134
The Poplar's Shadow 135
Working on Wall Street 136
Horses in Central Park 137
At East River 138
Four-Word Lines 139
While Seated in a Plane 140
The Tall Figures of Giacometti 141
August 19, Pad 19 142
The James Bond Movie 144
Face to Face (translation) 145
On the Road (translation) 146
Watching the Jets Lose to Buffalo at Shea 147
Women 148

Prison Architecture 149
Under the Baby Blanket 150
Sleeping with Boa 152
A Rescue 153
The Pure Suit of Happiness 155
A Wish 156
The Lowering 157
The Rest of My Life 158
Stripping and Putting On 160
The Exchange (first draft) 162

Index of Dates 163
Books by May Swenson 165
Awards Won by May Swenson 167

Foreword

By Richard Wilbur

May Swenson was not much given to self-absorption or self-portraiture, but in one of her later poems we find her looking at herself and seeing the lineaments of her mother and father. "I look at my hand," she says—

> I look at my hand and see
> it is also his and hers;
> the pads of the fingers his,
>
> the wrists and knuckles hers.
> In the mirror my pugnacious eye
> and ear of an elf, his;
>
> my tamer mouth and slant
> cheekbones hers.

That gives us a glimpse of May Swenson, though I should like to qualify it; she did indeed inherit a brow and set of eyes which were capable of pugnacity, but what I mostly saw in her blue eyes was forthrightness, independence, good nature, and a great power of attention. She had an appealing and sociable Swedish face, with fair hair cut in a "Dutch bob" across the forehead.

May's parents were converted to Mormonism, came over from Sweden and settled in Logan, Utah, and had ten children, of whom she was the eldest. After her graduation from the college where her father taught mechanical engineering, and after a spell of journalism in Utah, she came east and lived, for most of her writing life, in the New York area. Nevertheless, she remained Western in many ways. She had a great relish for wild nature and a knowing sympathy with wild creatures; her poems are full of tents and cabins and the out-of-doors; when an Amy Lowell fellowship took her to Europe for the first time, at the age of forty-seven, she and a companion "bought a small French car and tenting equipment" and, in their travels through France, Spain, and Italy, spent most of their nights under canvas. Effete Easterners do not make the grand tour in that fashion. The poems are Western, too, in their openness of tone and diction; even at their trickiest, they are made out of plain American words. The breezy spontaneity of their technique—the lineation and spacing, the playful random rhyming—makes sometimes for a lack of finish, but more usually seems in perfect accord with the swift vigor of her spirit.

One thing she did not bring east was Mormonism, or any other kind of church religion. This did not result in any sense of loss, or any want of scope. What May put in the place of any supernatural view was a truly knowledgeable awareness, rare among poets of our time, of the world as perceived and probed by contemporary science. An initial reaction to the mention of science, in connection with May's poetry, might be to think of her famous descriptive power, her ability to make us see objects sharply and in new ways: it was this talent which led Robert Lowell to say: "Miss Swenson's quick-eyed poems should be hung with permanent fresh-paint signs." When we talk about Marianne Moore or Elizabeth Bishop, we soon find ourselves quoting their brilliant captures and sightings of things, and so it is with May Swenson, who admired them both: one thinks of how, in a poem of May's, young skunk cabbages rise up out of a swamp like "Thumbs of old / gloves, the nails / poked through / and curled." Or one remembers the lines in which she conveys the shape, motion, and wake of an East River tugboat: "A large shoe / shuffles the floor of water, / leaving a bright scrape."

But this power to observe things keenly is not all that May Swenson shares with the scientist, as may be learned from an essay which she wrote for the *Voice of America* in the sixties, and entitled "The Experience of Poetry in a Scientific Age." What's central in that essay is its acceptance, as a model for poetry, of our cognitive situation as described by the atomic physicist, for whom the swarming particles which constitute the cosmos are not knowable in themselves, but are inevitably altered by our instruments of perception. If that is the way we know the universe, then the unit of reality is not an objective recording of data, or an imposition of order, but an occasion of interplay or dialogue between perceiver and world—what Whitehead called a "prehension." May's poetry is full of such moments of interplay-perceptual games and experiments in seeing which are grounded in a serious theory of knowledge. Her little poem, "Forest," for example, begins this way:

> The pines, aggressive as erect tails of cats,
> bob their tips when the wind freshens.

It then proceeds to depict the pine forest entirely in the key of cat—discovering a feline character in its brindled colors, its humped and springy floor, its lashed and winking boughs, and the purring sound of the wind going through them. This might seem merely a fanciful imposition, a virtuoso feat, were it not for the fact that the poet's accurate metaphors realize the forest more vividly than any botanist's language could do—so that the poet in her turn is acted upon, and the revealed strangeness of the scene creates in her a mood of forest-fear, of panic. The poem thus ends with these lines:

> My neck-hairs rise. The feline forest grins
>
> behind me. Is it about to follow?
> Which way out through all these whiskered yawns?

At the beginning of the essay to which I've referred, May Swenson says this about the poetic experience: "I see it based in a craving to get through the curtains of things as they *appear,* to things as they *are,* and then into the larger, wilder space of things as they are *becoming.*" That sentence contains the whole drama of May Swenson's poetry, the passion which underlies her playfulness. Though she knows that the senses can deceive us, it is through the alert, surprising use of those instruments that she seeks to break through to reality, refusing (as she says) "to take given designations for granted" or "to accept without a second look the name or category of a thing for the thing itself." Her poetry is, in fact, at war with names and designations, insofar as they can occlude our vision or foreclose our curiosity. God, she tells us in one of her poems, is a name which men have given to the idea of changelessness, and such a name is delusive in a world where everything moves and alters, where all is "breathing change." As for the lesser names—such as stream, flower, or roller-coaster—it is a special and frequent strategy of hers to withhold them, so that the poem may look more closely, naively, and inquiringly at the things to which they refer.

The riddle is an ancient poetic form in which an object is darkly described and its name withheld. May wrote a good many fine riddles about such objects as egg and fire and butterfly—enough so that a selection could be made "for young readers" and published in 1966 under the title of *Poems to Solve*. We are foolishly inclined nowadays to look at such poems as kid stuff; but to see May Swenson's riddles as part of her whole poetic enterprise is to rediscover the dignity of the form. Richard Howard was right to say that, in this aspect of her work, May wrote "a poetry that goes back to Orpheus." A riddle is at first a concealment, the withholding of a name; but as and when we solve its dark metaphor, the riddle is a revelation, giving us not only a name, but an object freed from clichés of perception and seen with wonder as if for the first time. Most of May's poems, of course, are not riddles, yet again and again they make use of riddling strategy to produce their revelations, and to enforce an intense participation in the reader. In a poem called "Motherhood," we seem at first to be looking at an unusually ugly naked woman, who is holding a skinny, louse-ridden child to her breast; yet by the end of the poem, when the mother is proudly swinging from bar to bar with the infant clinging to her armpit-hair, we have somehow been led to see her as beautiful. One reason for the success of the piece is that nowhere in title or text are we given such words as "ape" or "zoo" or "cage"—words which would allow us to relax into preconceptions. The poem is by no means obscure; one begins rather early to know the "answer"; and yet this withholding of a few clinching words prompts one to look hard at the object, be limber in one's response to it, and rejoice at last in another creature's splendid life.

That is what May meant by *getting through*, a process in which the poet transforms the object by some imaginative approach, draws closer to it by repeated acts of attention, and is at last, herself, transformed by the object. We have this pattern at its simplest in a poem called "While Seated on a Plane." There, the poet looks out of a plane-window and sees the cloudscape as a great parlor full of soft chairs and couches; she then dreams of walking out to make herself comfortable in that "celestial furniture," but is perplexed of course, by its vast, turbulent changes of form; the solution is a further act of imagination, in which she forsakes her own shape and substance, and conceives herself as perpetually "deformed and reformed." "One must be a cloud," as the poem says, "to occupy a house of cloud." Playful and charming as the poem is, it is like many another poem of May's in its passionate wish to cancel the distinction between subject and object, and to be at one with the portion of reality described. That is the impulse behind the "shaped poems" of which she wrote so many, and of which my favorite is a study of wave-behavior called "How Everything Happens." These creations, which dispose their words on the page to suggest the form or motion of the subject, represent not only pictorial wit but the desire of the poem to become what it is about.

Like Emily Dickinson, who much influenced her, May lived in the universe. No poet of our day has said and conjectured so much about stars and space. But whereas Dickinson's soul could expand to the limits of space and beyond, May's universe is ultimately that of the astronomer and physicist—a storm of galaxies and particles still uncharted by the mind, in which the mind itself may seem anomalous and lonely. Such a reality can be frightening, and May's poems have their moments of Pascalian dread; but her prevalent mood is one of delight. That needs no explaining, I think: when art is morose, we want to know why, but joy requires no reasons. It is clear, however, that she trusted her craving to get beyond the self, and her rapture in making imaginative fusions with the other. In consequence, her poems find the erotic in all forms of natural energy, and whether they speak of nebulae or horses or human love, are full of a wonderfully straightforward and ebullient sexuality. As for death, she approaches it often in a spirit of Whitmanian merging. Here are the opening lines of a sprightly later poem called "Ending":

> Maybe there *is* a Me inside of me
> and, when I lie dying, he
> will crawl out. Through my toe.
> Green on the green rug, and then

white on the wall, and then
over the windowsill, up the trunk
of the apple tree, he
will turn brown and rough and warty
to match the bark. . . .

She is poking fun, there, at conventional notions of the soul, but there is no missing the fact that blessedness, for her, would be a state of perfect transparency.

I don't know where May is now, but her poems continue to mix with time, and to be part of the vitality of the world.

Richard Wilbur and May Swenson at a Bryn Mawr College poetry reading in honor of Marianne Moore, 1976.

Chapter 1

To Utah!

From her earliest beginnings, May Swenson must have understood the freedom of words. Both of her parents kept a written memory of what they experienced leaving their homeland and emigrating to America long before their poet daughter was born.

"I had the most wonderful father and mother," Margaret Hellberg Swenson, May's mother, wrote in her autobiography.

> They were such sweethearts together. Mother worked so hard to have everything perfect. Father's work, in a steel factory, was hard with long hours, not too healthy either, and with very small pay. So mother decided to open a cafeteria. . . .
>
> My father's death was a terrible trial . . .
>
> In 1901 great things happened to us to change our lives. The Mormon missionaries found us. It was such a joy to have the elders come for a meal each week. Yes, I recall that often we were half-starved through the week so that we could have plenty of nice food for them when they came.
>
> I was twelve years old when five of us from our family were baptized. In those days and for many years, the Mormon Church was not a popular

Margaret Hellberg, May Swenson's mother, was born in Eskilstuna, Sweden, February 23, 1889. She clearly cherished the memory of her own parents.

Carl Henrik Hellberg and Anna Cristina Blomkvist, May's maternal grandparents, on their wedding day in Sweden. He died when May's mother was seven years old, leaving the family disconsolate as well as financially dependent on the hard work of their mother.

one in Sweden so all our relatives and friends turned against us.

Before I was fifteen I left home and lived in Stockholm where I obtained employment first as a housemaid. I worked for a lady who had a sewing center, making ladies' coats and suits. I took care of the apartment and also the cooking, washing, and special house cleaning along with delivering the clothing she had produced. . . . My employer felt that she treated me royally when she invited me to eat at her table, though she just gave me some scraps that she did not care for: a hard crust of bread and sour milk and at times a bit of old leftovers while she had the fresh cooked food, which I had prepared.

My pay was six crowns a month, about one dollar and twenty-five cents. I had saved to get some gifts for my younger brothers and sisters and for Mother and for the boat trip home to Eskilstuna. Well, the day before Christmas Eve I worked extra hard on the holiday cleaning. There were breads and sweet rolls to bake. As I took a dozen cardamom rolls out of the oven the mistress counted them carefully into a large tin can and carried them to her room to store in her cupboard, which she always kept locked. . . .

While living in Stockholm I was a housemaid in three different homes and a waitress for a while. I worked in an old folks home and in a fancy store where

Margaret Hellberg, in her apron, serving tea to her employer's aristocratic friends.

the royal family came to buy wine, fruit, and candy of all kinds. This store was in the fashionable part of town. The manager helped me get work in a hospital where I worked from age eighteen to twenty-two.

—from Margaret Hellberg Swenson's unpublished autobiography

Margaret Hellberg posed for this formal photograph before she left for her new life in America. She was twenty-three, bound for Utah to marry Dan Arthur Swenson, whom she had met while he was serving as a Mormon missionary in Stockholm.

After Dan was released from his mission and left Sweden for Utah he wrote to me every day telling me of his love so I knew that he felt we should not wait to get married since he was already thirty-two years old. . . . I had planned to take a job in Utah and learn the ways and customs of my new country first. Dan claimed that he had waited long enough for me.

—from Margaret's autobiography

Dan and Margaret Swenson settled in Logan soon after their marriage. She stayed home with her domestic responsibilities, did church work, and in 1913, gave birth to

Main Street in the college town of Logan, Utah, about 1919.

Dan and Margaret Swenson in 1940.

May, the first of her ten children. Dan started his long career teaching at Utah Agricultural College, the present-day Utah State University.

Margaret wrote, "I can truly say that we two were always sweethearts . . . a team working together to provide for our children's future. My wonderful husband was a perfect manager, hard working, resourceful, industrious from his youth on."

Dan Arthur Swenson was born in the school house at Roena, Osby, Kristianstad Province, Sweden, on November 8, 1880, to Swen Swenson and Thilda Pehrson Swenson. Dan, too, wrote an autobiography:

> I was the fifth child in a family of ten. My father was away from home on some business connected with his school work—he was a teacher—when I arrived, and when he returned home and Mother showed him the new baby he exclaimed, "*Sadan enfuling!*" (What a homely one!) A handicap that I never grew out of!
>
> As there were so many more boys than girls in the family we could not be discriminating as to the kind of work we should do so I learned to darn and knit and some sewing, too. I learned to mix and knead the dough for rye bread, tend

Birthplace of Dan Arthur Swenson.

the baby and change didies, and many, many other things. There was no time to be idle and not much time for playing in order to exist in Sweden in those days. Everyone had to work. The world of today has little idea of the wonders of handicraft that were wrought in many a humble home in those days. . . . I recall how, as children, we would go with Mother out in the surrounding woodland and gather leaf-covered branches, tie them in small bundles, and when the leaves were dried, store them away for the winter. They were then used to eke out the feed for the sheep, who greedily munched on the dry leaves and twigs. Then, when the sheep had been sheared, Mother would take the wool, card it into slender rolls about 3¼ inches in diameter, and spin it on her wheel into soft, white or gray yarn. During every spare moment she knit stockings, mittens, and mufflers for the family. . . .

Then sudden misfortune engulfed us when Father lost his teaching job. One week we lived happily in comfort in the school house, the next week we had no home and no income. . . . When things got so bad that we had nothing to eat, the local authorities felt impelled to step in and see what could be done. There was no poorhouse in the locality, at least no place where children could be

A view of the Wasatch Front in northern Utah, part of the Rocky Mountain Range.

> cared for, so the only solution in such cases was an auction to dispose of or provide for the children. . . . The thoughts of the family being disintegrated, losing parents and brothers and sisters and going to live with strangers brought such terror to my heart it cannot be described with words.
>
> —from Dan Arthur Swenson's unpublished autobiography

Mormon missionaries were now the Swenson's only friends. They baptized the family and then helped them emigrate to America. Dan continues his story:

> We landed in New York in September, 1894, and I was frightened out of my wits, for I was left on a bench in the railroad station while Mother went out to buy provisions for the five days' train journey to Utah. . . . It was a happy day when one of the missionaries pointed out a hazy outline on the horizon and told us "Those are the Rocky Mountains. When we get there we will be in Zion."
>
> —from Dan's autobiography

Dan was soon earning his own living doing farm work in Utah. Later he toiled on a railroad gang and on a road-construction crew pouring concrete. He wrote:

Dan Arthur Swenson in his ROTC uniform at Utah Agricultural College.

Dan Arthur at the band saw in the Mechanical Arts Building of Utah Agricultural College. Along with his academic subjects he registered for woodwork classes.

It was hard to keep going all day long, work that made me determined to go to college. Yet I was never afraid of work. I have been known to lie down by it at night and sleep.

I became acquainted with Neils L. Monson who had spent a short time as a student at Utah Agricultural College. He told me that at that school one could obtain a good education and also learn a trade. . . . The seed had been planted and by and by it began to grow.

—from Dan's autobiography

In September, 1901, Dan Swenson entered Utah Agricultural College as a freshman. He had the equivalent of only a fifth-grade education so had to struggle to catch up, while at the same time working as a handyman at the college dormitory. He recalls:

Old Main at Utah Agricultural College in the year Dan Arthur Swenson graduated, 1907.

Occasionally our assignment for the English class would be to write a poem. Such an assignment was often tackled with a good deal of trepidation. How could a body who had barely learned to speak the English language in a halting way dare to attempt poetry? Besides, our teacher used to say, "Oh, you are such an unsophisticated lot!" I didn't know what that word meant, but judging by her expression I didn't think it was meant for a compliment. However, I thought, "If it's poetry you want, you shall have it."

OH SAVE NOT THE ROSE

Oh save not the rose till thy friend has departed,
To lay it, as emblem of love, on his grave,
But give it today to a friend broken-hearted,
To cheer his sad spirit, to make his heart brave.

Oh spare not the praise you so freely are giving
To those who have passed from this troublesome sphere;
But lend it to brighten the days for the living,
To call forth new efforts from those who are near.

Oh stay not thy hand till thy help is required
To carry thy kin to the last resting place,
But give thy aid gladly, whenever desired,
Then Mankind will bless thee, and God give thee grace.

Dan Swenson's graduation project, a carved oak cellarette, won a silver medal at the Utah State Fair, 1907.

. . . It was a rule in the woodwork department to have each student select a piece of furniture to make as a graduating piece during the last year. I chose to make a cellarette out of quartered oak, with carved pieces and an elaborately carved panel for a door. I spent considerable time producing the design for the carving, and I am sure that my plan contemplated the most elaborate piece of carving ever attempted at the college at that time, and, for that matter, since that time, if I do say so myself.

—from Dan's autobiography

Two years after graduation, Dan returned to Sweden as a Mormon missionary. At church in Stockholm he heard Margaret Hellberg singing in the choir. "She was by far the best alto. She sang herself right into my heart. After I returned to Utah I sent for Margaret. Though we were actually separated only six months, it seemed like an eternity for I loved her so much."

They were married on August 21, 1912, and Dan began a new job as assistant in the woodwork department at Utah Agricultural College. Soon, they started a family.

Our first baby, Anna Thilda May, was born at 2:30 A.M. on Wednesday, May 28, 1913. I remember so well going out in the street to guide Dr. E. S. Budge into the house. I went hurriedly ahead and on looking back found the doctor sprawled on the ground. He had not noticed in the dark that there was an open ditch in front of the place. In spite of the delay, May came into the world safe and sound and what a bonny lass she proved to be.

—from Dan's autobiography

May and her father.

Chapter 2

Love at Home

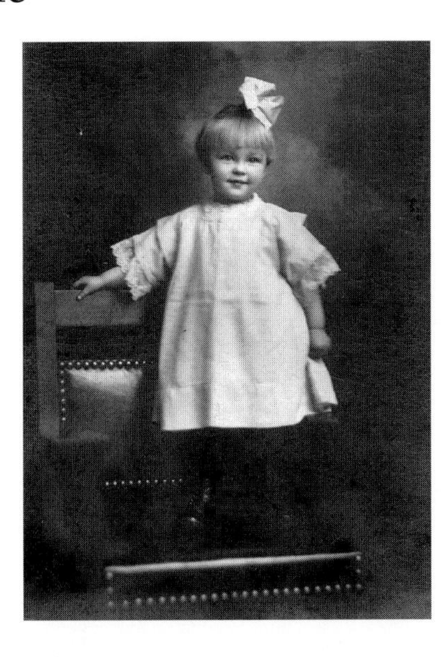

May wearing "a faint but cocky smile."

In her first formal photograph May stands on a chair her father had made in his workshop at Utah Agricultural College. "How proud we were of our beautiful child," he wrote. May later described a similar photo in her poem, "The Desk. The Body."

> In little over-ankle, square-toed black shoes you stand
> on the leather seat of the armchair, left hand curled
> on its back. . . .
> A faint but cocky smile
> on your prissy little lips, confidence gleams
> in your narrow eyes, and already one eyebrow, the left,
> is pixily raised higher than the other.
> You have fat cheeks and a tiny button nose,

May's father made her a buggy so she could push her rag doll around the yard of their small rented house at 495 North 600 East. There were two bedrooms upstairs, two rooms downstairs—a parlor and a kitchen. There was no indoor plumbing. Water was drawn from a hydrant to fill a bucket that always stood inside the kitchen door. A wooden walk led to the outhouse, and an irrigation canal bisected the property, which was partially fenced with wooden pickets. Poplar trees grew on the other side of the fence. Old Main on campus can be seen in the distance.

a level straight-forward stare,
narrow Swedish eyes neither offering nor asking—
just alert, intently observing.

May's brother Dan describes childhood joys:

The streetcar went by our house twice an hour. We used to pick up soda water bottle caps at the neighborhood grocery store and put them on the car tracks to be run over by the streetcar. We used the flattened caps for play money. Wild camomile grew along and between the car tracks and we harvested and dried it for tea, which Dad called "car-track tea."

In the wintertime Dad would build a roaring fire in the heating stove in the upstairs bedroom to warm things up for bedtime. Sometimes he would bake apples over the hot coals in the stove to give us a treat before going off to sleep. The room would be warm and cozy when we were tucked in but by morning the glass of water on the window sill would be frozen into ice.

On Easter we always went up on College Hill to roll our colored eggs down the hill. Seagulls would appear from nowhere and clean up the broken eggs and

In prose pieces about her childhood May described her mother at the washing machine doing the growing family's huge laundry. May wrote about the smell of white clothes hanging on the backyard lines and the tents the Swenson children made by pinning the "sides of sheets to the ground with nails from Dad's tool box."

The Swensons, dressed in their Sunday school best: May with her brothers Dan, born in 1916, and Roy, born in 1915.

bits of sandwiches from picnics. On one Easter we had very bad weather. Dad went up to his shop on campus and built a long chute from a wide board with strips on the edges. He brought this home and put it on the stairway. We rolled our eggs from upstairs to downstairs.

"My father was a handyman around the house," May wrote years later in a story she called "Appetite." She listed the chores her father would do: "Darn socks, peel pears, make rootbeer and cider, gather tomatoes, pick raspberries, dry apples and corn, prune fruit trees, keep bees." In the poem "Something Goes By," she noted:

My dad built our house, poured concrete for the basement,
sawed timber for the frame, laid the brick,
put on the roof, shingle by shingle,
lying along the ladder with nails in his mouth,

May's father holds his baby son George, born in 1917. May and Dan perch alongside, while Roy leans over the back of the chair.

plastered the inside, laid the floorboards,
made our furniture out of wood:
of wave-grained oak our dining table . . .
my round, high stool he scooped in the center just like a saucer . . .

May's sister Margaret recalls their Christmas feasts:

> With Mother's honey wheat bread and Swedish *limpa,* we enjoyed condiments such as *gurka* and pickled beets and lingonberry jam. The fish were sardines, anchovies on hard-boiled eggs, salmon, and pickled herring in sour cream, May's favorite. And lutfish, dried cod shipped from Scandinavia. Dad would soak it in lye water before it could be cooked. Our dessert was always *ris-grins gröt*—a delicate rice pudding cooked all day in a double boiler in a creamy milk and sprinkled with cinnamon and sugar. With the pudding, we had Mother's *kaffe*

The Swenson house at 669 East 500 North stood one hundred yards from the campus. Each Christmas the boys and their father designed decorations, rigged lights to blink on and off, dyed the light bulbs many colors—and won contests for their efforts.

The Swensons celebrated Christmas in the Swedish tradition. On Jul Afton, Christmas Eve, they decorated the tree and danced around it singing "Now it is Christmas again." In this Christmas photo May holds the hand of her sister Grace, born in 1921. May's father holds Ruth, born in 1922, and her mother holds new baby Beth, born in 1923.

> *bullar*, coffee rolls spiced with cardamom. Before we could eat dessert, we had to recite a little verse in Swedish that we had spent the day composing.

For the big Swenson family, May had much housework and cooking to do. She helped "put up" fruit and vegetables to store in the cellar under the front porch. She washed thousands of dishes in the sink her father had placed low for the children to use. She helped with the family laundry, using a "wringerless and savage" washer, then ironed her brothers' shirts hundreds of times over the years. Their work outside in the garden and orchard was what she'd rather have been doing.

As a child May's best friend was Muriel Morris. She lived in a small clapboard house next door to the Swensons. "In summertime we spent hours playing jacks and jumping rope," Muriel has written.

The flag was always hung for holidays at 669 East 500 North, here in 1923.

Muriel Morris.

In the evenings, with May's brothers and others in the neighborhood, we played kick-the-can. We both liked to read and enjoyed reading to each other. When we were in fifth and sixth grades, our teacher, Mrs. Phillips, took a real interest in May and encouraged her in her talent. May's father taught woodworking at the college and we used to roam the halls of Old Main. We always went to the museum, which I remember had displays of animal and insect kingdoms. May was not a person who found it easy to show her feelings but the feelings were there and I always knew of her friendship and loyalty.

After being out of touch for many years, Muriel wrote to May in 1969, describing her life in Rigby, Idaho. May answered

Dear Muriel: Those were innocent times—I mean our childhood—and it was an innocent era, the first quarter of this century. And we were in an innocent place and society—the church out there in Utah. . . . You are still who you were except that your life has been added upon, having had, as you say, perhaps a very ordinary life as wife, mother, and grandmother, and what a triumph to be able to write "but it has been very satisfying to me." That's it, that's all—that's the

At Webster Elementary School May was a "splendid student," according to her teacher, Mrs. Phillips. She wrote on May's report card: "You have been blessed with good parents, a real home, and I hope you will do something fine in the world."

May's childhood friend, LaNorma Jensen, who lived two houses west of the Swensons, remembers that May spent "hours hidden in the thick willows across the street reading, not books of trivia but profound books, books of inspiration and learning."

May in costume. Behind her is the Eccles Caine's horse pasture, and in the distance, the women's dorm on College Hill.

M. I. A. TO GIVE DANCE

Toe Dancing by S. L. Girl Will Be Feature

Interpretive Numbers Are Included in Program

One of the features of the annuall "Green and Gold" ball of the Liberty ward Young Men's and Young Women's Mu-

Miss Edna Swenson, one of the feature entertainers for the Liberty ward "Green and Gold" ball, who will give a toe dance on Thursday night.

will give her interpretative "In Poppy Land" dance as a part of the

May's cousin Sunny was the first to pronounce May a poet.

definition of success and happiness—that's the total, no one can get more, and few in all the mass of mankind past and present, I suspect, obtain it.

At about twelve years of age May began keeping a diary. Her father had made her twenty little books with blank pages. "I would discuss with myself what was happening inside me," May later told an interviewer. One day, May showed a page to her older cousin Edna—nicknamed "Sunny"—who read the page aloud, noticed that the sentences scanned, and remarked that May was writing poetry in her diary.

"But I have never thought of myself as a poet, the way kids do nowadays," May often said later.

For a time Sunny lived in the Swenson's basement apartment and gave dancing lessons in Logan. May took part in Sunny's recitals, as did other Swenson children.

May giving her baby sister Beth a ride.

May also acted in and directed plays for the Mutual Improvement Association, a Mormon church organization for young people. For one production, May persuaded her father to cut a hole in the stage so she could stand with her feet in it to play a grave digger. May's friend LaNorma Jensen was in the audience for "The Grave Digger." She writes:

> All the church wards performed the same play. After so much of the same it became boring. The Logan Fifth Ward, our ward, was last. May literally held the audience spellbound when she threw the last shovel of dirt. Many of us felt a personal victory.

The Fifth Ward took first place in the contest and everyone in the cast won a pin.

May's sisters and brothers knew her better as a storyteller than as a poet. Beth remembers the stories May would make up as she gave the sisters Dutch haircuts. Ruth numbers among her choicest memories the many times May entertained the younger children as she scrubbed the kitchen floor. These stories often related to things that were taking place in the family. Ruth writes:

> I vividly recall one time when I was about seven years old. I sat cross-legged at the kitchen doorway. May, on all fours, backed away from me as she scrubbed. I was admiring my new shoes and feeling a special love for my daddy, who that morning had taken me and Beth and Grace to town and bought all three of us new shoes. He had paid ninety-eight cents for each pair. Three dollars was hard to come by at the beginning of the Great Depression. I'm sure May realized this much better than I did. She told the story of a centipede who had ten children and all of them needed shoes. She helped me figure out the logistics—ten children, each with one hundred feet, equals one thousand feet or five hundred pairs of shoes!

The Swenson's first car was a used 1914 Studebaker touring sedan. Here, in 1926, May is thirteen years old, wearing her hair in a long braid twisted around her head—a "halo" according to her brother Roy, who wrote:

> *May sits in front of Dan, age 10, on the hot hood one June noon, towering over me, age 11. An apprentice mom, May was babysitter, maid, and storyteller and also she echoed Dad's quiet, gentle wisdom when, on occasion, she was left in charge of us children. To my left on the running board sit Eccles Caine, a neighbor, and Grace, Beth, Ruth, and George. Mother, coaxed from her many pressing duties to pose, said to Dad, "I don't have time, but I'll come when you're all ready, if you insist."*

Grace remembers her big sister May as "a personage of authority."

> I felt very small. Hers was the rank of privilege—firstborn. There existed this trio of "other creatures" between us—the boys—and they were often under her jurisdiction, as, of course, was I. What an awesome and unbidden responsibility for her! She handled it with some resigned reluctance but it was a given and she gave herself, as was her lot, exercising high creativity along with a quiet sense of reserve.

May (right) with Helen Richards (left) and Verdena Vickers (center) in Logan Canyon at a summer camp sponsored by the Mutual Improvement Association.

May as a high school student.

May was the babysitter also for LaNorma Jensen on nights when Mrs. Jensen was away on nursing assignments. LaNorma remembers kneeling down beside her bed for evening prayers with May. "Being a novice at praying, it didn't take me long, but May prayed on and on. May had such pretty hands. I marveled at their beauty, considering all the tons of dishes May washed at home."

May, Helen Richards, and Muriel Morris called themselves "The Three Musketeers." They attended movies together, participated in church activities, and helped each other with their studies at Logan High School.

"Helen was busy with shorthand and typing. At noon we ate our sack lunches together and often dictated to Helen so that she could practice her shorthand on the

Cast photo, "The Rejuvenation of Aunt Mary," from The Buzzer *yearbook. May is in the top row, third from the right.*

blackboard," Muriel has written. "Helen was a strong, spiritual person. May had great admiration for her."

As a Christmas gift in 1928, Helen gave May a book of Mormon doctrine, *Added Upon*, by Nephi Anderson. Judging from the many underlined passages, question marks, and jottings in the margins, May must have read the book carefully and no doubt discussed it with her friends. May underlined "The tangled threads of earth-life are not all straightened out yet," and added her own conclusion: "Sometime, somewhere we'll understand."

An early prize of May's was for a story contest at Logan High School. Her "Christmas Day" won $25.00, the Vernon Short Story Medal, and was published in the school's newspaper in 1929.

At the Utah State Agricultural College (1930-34), May's interest in acting and play production continued. As a freshman she had a part in the play "The Rejuvenation of Aunt Mary," and spent twenty-five hours without a break painting scenery for the play.

May, a sophomore in college.

Logo for May's column in Student Life.

As a sophomore May began writing for *Student Life,* the campus newspaper. Listed on the masthead as "Humor Writer," she wrote paragraph fillers, some of them in student slang of the day. When her first poem was published in the campus literary magazine, *The Scribble,* a fellow student wrote, "The cadence, tone, and imagery of May Swenson's 'Three Hues of Melody' was distinctly individual and fantastic. Miss Swenson shows promise."

As a junior and senior May wrote a humorous column, "Station Hooey," for *Student Life*. The form and content seem to have been suggested by radio programs of the day. May had been listening to the radio for years.

"We had one of the first radios in Logan. It had earphones. We lined up to use them," May's sister Ruth recalls.

Their father built a wooden cabinet for the radio. One spring when the roads were clear of snow, they drove to Salt Lake City and gave the radio to Grandfather Swenson, who had been a lifetime reader but was blind in old age. The Swenson children got it back when their grandfather died in 1925.

May's closest friend at college was Edith Welch. They were introduced at a *Scribble* meeting at the home of Austin Fife, who became a well-known folklorist. Ray B. West, Jr. was also there. He'd brought along

May as a senior in college. Edith Welch remembers her as "chubby."

May and Edith Welch on campus, prepared for a picnic up Logan Canyon.

a copy of Joyce's *Ulysses*, and the group of scribblers read it together. West had already written a novel of his own. He went on to found the *Rocky Mountain Review* and published several of May's poems there.

During Edith's sophomore year she got better acquainted with May. Edith has said (in an interview):

> May and I talked endlessly. I would come feeling burdened to May, who was always comforting. She took the long view. "Wait until tomorrow," she would say. Our friendship grew. We sang in a chorus. May had a good voice

> and loved a song called *Listen to the Lambs All A-Crying*. My junior year, May invited me to come and stay in her "studio" at her parents' home. I paid her father $3.00 a month for the privilege and boarded across the street for another $20.00 a month. May's family was good to me. Her mother seemed to me even then to be hard put to know how to treat her intelligent, imaginative daughter. She wanted all five of her girls to lead normal lives in the Mormon church, and May didn't seem to be fitting into the pattern. Her friends at the college were the "wrong crowd"—slightly "pink" and critical of the Mormon faith.

At home May never openly opposed her family's faith. She didn't ask "Why should I go to church?" She didn't come home from Sunday meetings and criticize what she'd seen and heard.

"May was respectful of anything our parents did," her sister Beth has written.

Yet to her friends at the college May confided "It's not for me—religion. It seems like a redundancy for a poet." Edith continues:

> May and I used to visit our *Scribble* friend Gladys Hobbs at her office at the *Herald Journal* in Logan. We did a little writing for the *Herald* and earned a little money. Gladys would read us funny things sent in by people. We'd rock with laughter. Later on, Gladys moved to Salt Lake and I got married. May moved to New York. She felt she had to get away from Utah, make her own way, not be dependent on anyone.

Other lasting friendships May made at *Scribble* meetings were with fellow poets Veneta Nielsen and Grant Redford, who both became English professors. Some believed May was crazy about Grant, who, according to Veneta, was "romantically handsome, magnetic of temperament, and seemed a drama all by himself." Certainly May and Grant corresponded until his death by suicide in 1965. May answered a fan letter from Grant (in 1955) by saying she was thrilled he had read a published story of hers to his class. Veneta, too, used May's work in her classes at their alma mater and invited May back to Logan to read her poems there.

The Mormon Temple in Logan.

"When May spoke in my classes, everything was fresh," Veneta remembers. "My students asked May to name her favorite American poet.

"'If I liked any poetry better than my own, wouldn't I try to write that way?' May answered."

May sometimes walked to the Logan Temple to sit on the rolling lawn overlooking Cache Valley and write poems. One day there she decided she'd outgrown her "pure and boring" hometown. She persuaded her parents to let her move to Salt Lake City to live with Sunny at Uncle Ren's. May found a job there soliciting advertisements for a newspaper and plunged into Sunny's social whirl. But by the summer of 1936, they were both on a Greyhound bus traveling east. They picked up Sunny's new car at a factory in Michigan and from there drove on to New York, Sunny for a visit, May to live in the city she knew only from Steiglitz photos and Thomas Wolfe's novel, *Of Time and the River*.

May left behind in Utah this poem published in the anthology *Utah Sings* in 1934:

CREATION

It is a stern thing,
This bringing into being;
This taking of a clod that is cold
And veining it with sprouts of fire;
This wresting of a star from chaos,
And chiseling it upon the lathe of exactness;
This making of an indolent thing urgent;
This begetting of eagerness;
It is a hard and a fierce thing . . .
Did You find it so, God?

May and Sunny traveling together.

Chapter 3

New York, New York

May had borrowed two hundred dollars from her father to pay for her cross-country "lark." He hadn't tried to dissuade her because she'd not announced her real intention: to live and work in New York "forever." In the diary she began on her arrival, May wrote she wanted to find herself out, find others who would understand her, and, above all, she wanted to learn to "create beauty." These were to be her goals during the Depression years of the late 1930s.

"So life in New York, come whirl me, come twirl me, life," May wrote.

When she was unable to get a job as a newspaper reporter, May advertised as a writer's helper, and after many interviews with "crackpots" she found "bosses" who paid her small sums as an editor and ghostwriter. One of these (she called him "Plat") became her boyfriend in the fall of 1936.

"I think I should like to have a son by Plat. . . . He would have Plat's long dark lashes and my oblique eyes. . . . But I would not like to be married to any man, but only be myself," May wrote in her diary.

Another boss was Anzia Yezierska, a fiction writer of the 1920s whose novels had been made into films. Now living in a shabby apartment in Greenwich Village, she seemed as destitute as May was getting to be. May typed parts of Anzia's autobiography and ran small errands for her, accepting the meager payment she

Anzia Yezierska and her daughter Louise in Washington Square Park.

offered. May was too proud to write home for money or to turn to her cousin Clyde, a lawyer living in Queens, New York. Instead, she moved from one closet-sized apartment to another—moved at the request of landladies to whom she owed rent.

May did visit Clyde and his wife Edna on Sundays for dinner and church services, even though May's Mormon faith had been slipping away for years. Eventually, she would give up attending church except when she was home in Logan and accompanied her parents. Yet she never asked to be stricken from the rolls of the church, nor was she excommunicated—merely considered "inactive" by the Manhattan Ward. A careful reading of the body of her work reveals her questioning of Mormon beliefs, but not complete rejection of her parents' faith.

Anzia's nephew, Arnold Kates, began going out with May in August, 1937. He worked in advertising, had a large apartment in the village, and a convertible runabout. Their usual dates were for movies, plays, and art galleries, but they also went hiking on the Palisades, went horseback riding, bowling, and played ping pong. May borrowed Arnold's books—Freud, Jung, Joyce, Huxley, e. e. cummings. She cleaned his apartment to earn enough money for her own rent.

Arnold Kates.

One day she was down to her last eighteen cents. "Marry Arnold and you won't have to worry about a place to live," Anzia suggested.

"I won't marry Arnold. This is so I will remember," May wrote in her diary.

Arnold may have been the first to take May to see the ocean—to Jones Beach and Southampton, Long Island. Her fascination with the tidal water appears in an unpublished short story she wrote in 1938:

"I am looking at the sea for the first time," Norma thought, seeing far out the heaving luminous plane lifting and falling in the tide. The water slipped up and creamed around her ankles and she looked near, watching in fascination the glassy green coil of water roaring upon her. Reaching her, it shattered and was

> sucked back carrying the sand from under her feet so that she seemed to be sinking and leaning out after the wave. And before she could move, another fierce coil of water caught her gasping.

May and Arnold broke off their relationship by friendly agreement. He later married and had a daughter, Barbara, who recalls his reading May's poems to her as a child.

It was probably Anzia who suggested that May go on relief and then apply for a job with the Federal Writers' Project. To certify as "indigent" and thus be eligible for this WPA program, May would have to claim she had no relatives, no insurance, no money. She did so knowing full well her father had the means to support her and would if she'd let him know of her poverty.

May, at left, with four other writers who found work in the Federal Writers' Project during the Depression. (May did not note on the photo the names of the other writers.)

An interview with Anca Vrbovska led to a lasting friendship. Above, May and Anca relax at Arthur's Tavern in Greenwich Village.

Before her lie was detected by a relief officer who tracked down May's Aunt Marie, she worked a year for the Living Lore Unit of the Federal Writers Project. She interviewed working-class people in New York City—postal telegraph workers, marine radio operators, drugstore employees, and department store workers among them. She typed her interviews and turned them in, never to hear a word about her work until 1980, when a collection of interviews was dug from the National Archives and published. (See *First Person America* by Ann Banks. May's interview, "Irving Fajans," is included.)

Anca Vrbovska, a writer May interviewed, had immigrated from Czechoslovakia to the United States as a young woman, to become, according to the Preface to her book *The Gate Beyond the Sun,* the "first Slovak poet to write poetry in English." She had married a baker, but was separated from him and living alone when, in October, 1938, she and May decided to pool their skimpy wages and rent a tiny apartment in the Village. They moved several times in years to come, ending up at 39 Bedford Street for seven years in the 1940s.

Anca on the roof at 39 Bedford Street. May nicknamed Anca "Frankie."

Coney Island was only a subway token away from the city. (Anca, left, May in the middle.) In her diary, Anca wrote "May loves the ocean."

May on the roof at 119 Bank Street. The apartment had two rooms and a bath for $30.00 a month.

Anca's diary for 1938-39 notes that May was "slender and blonde, with a very pale face, blue eyes, calm, almost cold appearance. . . . Shy of speech. . . . Ambitious, conscientious. . . . Her humor is dry, cutting, subtle." Anca further describes her own "feeling of peace due to May's presence."

May and Anca had little money to spare from rent and food but occasionally scraped enough together for a movie in the Village or a ballet uptown. May wrote to her brother George: "Last night Frankie and I went to the Ballet Russe at the Metropolitan Opera House. Paid $3.30 for seats in the 8th row orchestra and were terribly disappointed! I'm afraid the

"May Swenson" by Hans Bohler, circa 1938.

May as a student in sculpture class.

ballet is dying of old age—old dancers, old repertoires, lousy staging, and bad directing. We expected to be thrilled by some vestige of the spirit of the great Nijinsky but there was nothing there of that—in fact the performance was ridiculous, and we had a hard time keeping from laughing aloud, thus shocking the snooty socialites in evening gowns and tuxedos all around us."

At home, May and Anca read Kafka, Werfel, Blake, Poe, Donne, *The Magic Mountain,* and *The Daily Worker*, the newspaper of the American Communist Party. Anca was a devoted member and tried to convince May to join the party. May was certainly sympathetic to some of the party's ideas, especially to the idea of wealth-sharing that no doubt reminded May of Mormon welfare programs she had seen provide for families in Utah. But to May, the Communist Party leaders were "a pack of

Joe Doakes Turns Artist

THE LAYMAN LEARNS TO SCULP FOR A DOLLAR

An article in Click magazine described the class as "Art, not ART."

Alfred Kreymborg as a student in Saul Baizerman's class.

Saul Baizerman and his wife Eugenie.

"Man with the Shovel" by Saul Baizerman. May deeply admired his work and befriended his family.

dimwits." She did belong to a union, the Workers Alliance, Local 87, and took part in union demonstrations, but she preferred to use her free time "making art for art's sake": writing poetry and reading it at the Raven Poetry Club and taking a sketching class from the artist Hans Bohler, who used May for his model.

In 1941 May took a sculpture class from Saul Baizerman, whose work she'd seen in a Village gallery. One of May's classmates was the noted poet, playwright, and editor, Alfred Kreymborg, whose help with publishing her poems May was to seek years later.

SNOW IN NEW YORK

It snowed in New York. I walked on Fifth
Avenue and saw the orange snowplow cut the drifts
with rotary sickles, suck up celestial clods into its turning neck,
a big flue that spewed them into a garbage truck.
This gift from the alps was good for nothing, though scarcely gray.

The bright apparatus, with hungry noise,
crumbled and mauled the new hills. Convoys
of dump-cars hauled them away.

I went to Riker's to blow my nose
in a napkin and drink coffee for its steam. Two rows
of belts came and went from the kitchen, modeling scrambled
eggs, corn muffins, bleeding triangles of pie.
Tubs of dirty dishes slid by.
Outside the fogged window black bulking people stumbled
cursing the good-for-nothing whiteness. I thought
of Rilke, having read how he wrote

to Princess Marie von Thurn und Taxis, saying: "The idea haunts me—
it keeps on calling—I must make a poem for Nijinski
that could be, so to say, swallowed and then danced." Printed
as on the page, in its
remembered place in the paragraph, that odd name with three dots
over the *iji*, appeared—as I squinted
through the moist window past the traveling
dishes—against the snow. There unraveled

from a file in my mind a magic notion
I, too, used to play with: from chosen words a potion
could be wrung; pickings of them, eaten, could make you fly, walk
on water, be somebody else, do or undo anything, go back
or forward on belts of time. But then I thought:
Snow in New York is like poetry, or clothes made of roses.
Who needs it, what can you build with snow, who can you feed? Hoses
were coming to whip back to water, wash to the sewers the nuisance-freight.

Letters, photographs, and Christmas packages of Swedish food from home helped May survive the homesickness she felt during her first years in New York. Then visits from her brothers and sisters became possible when she moved to an apartment with a couch. May's brother George and other Mormon missionaries in

Thanksgiving Eve in Logan, 1939, May's fourth Thanksgiving away from home. Her youngest brother Paul is seated between his father and his sister Margaret.

On the way to Sweden for his Mormon mission, May's brother George took a walk with her around Central Park in 1938.

Europe returned to America when war seemed certain. George continued his mission in New Jersey. May wrote to him there in April, 1940: "It must be a shock for you to realize that these beautiful countries which you have recently been traveling in are now about to be blasted to bits by both German and English bombs." She also wrote about her job with the United States Travel Bureau:

> I have been doing good work and plenty of it and my boss admits he hasn't any complaints. When you were here I had a desk in the front, you remember? Then I was shifted again to the switchboard desk for a while, and just the other day shifted again to the department in the back where I now have a desk and am in charge of the poster files and correspondence, photo correspondence, current-events file, and general departmental typing. I like this spot best of the three.

The Swenson family, taken during May's visit to Logan in May, 1941.

With few civilians traveling because of the war, May soon found herself out of work again, and her next job—at J. Widder and Co., Exclusive Creations—proved less than secure. In April, 1941, she wrote George:

> I got fired today! This job turned out to be some sort of a racket and I couldn't stand it, had a row with the boss who is a complete moron, and so to my immense relief got the gate. Had been with them two weeks. But I have a good job lined up at $25.00 per week and so all's well that ends well.

When George was released from his mission in New Jersey, May drove back to Utah with him for her first home visit since she'd left there for New York.

"We had a gloriously happy motor trip from eastern U.S. to the West," George has written. "At one point we were traveling through Nebraska at approximately 80 miles an hour, and, as we were approaching a small town, May said, 'Gee, that's a pretty little town we're coming to, wasn't it?'"

May's sister Margaret also stayed with her at 39 Bedford Street. Margaret writes:

May and her sister Margaret on a cruise up the Hudson River during Margaret's month living with May in New York.

> May persuaded Dad to let me come and stay with her and Anca in the summer of 1946 and take a course at the Traphagen School of Art and Design in downtown Manhattan. May said my board and room would be free. Her apartment had only one bedroom but there was a studio couch in the living room where I could sleep and a screened-off kitchenette with the smallest undercounter refrigerator I'd ever seen; also a "built-in" cat named "Jungle Boy." May always had a cat. There were cases with lots of books.
>
> That summer I read *Strange Fruit* and for the first time I learned how black people had been persecuted in the South. I got a conscience. We were on a bus with Anca one day and when she asked for change the driver said, "Damn Jew." Anca was very, very angry but told me it had happened before.
>
> The Sunday after I arrived May took me out to dinner at an Italian restaurant with real red-checked tablecloths and real Italian waiters. Monday morning May and I rode the 'A' train. She helped me register at Traphagen, then left for work after giving me instructions on how to get home. She bought me a set of pastel chalks and encouraged me all the way. She took me to an opera, to musicals, to the ballet, on a cruise up the Hudson, to Jones Beach and to all kinds of restaurants. We even ate clams on the half shell from pushcarts on Bleeker Street.

RIDING THE "A"

I ride
the "A" train
and feel
like a ball-
bearing in a roller skate.
I have on a gray
rain-
coat. The hollow
of the car
is gray.
My face
a negative in the slate
window,
I sit
in a lit
corridor that races
through a dark
one. Strok-
ing steel,
what a smooth rasp—it feels
like the newest of knives
slicing
along
a long
black crusty loaf
from West 4th to 168th.
Wheels
and rails
in their prime
collide,

Margaret's photo of May, top of the Empire State Building.

make love in a glide
of slickness
and friction.
It is an elation
I wish to pro-
long.
The station
is reached
too soon.

Grace Swenson, May's sister, on the beach at Santa Monica, California.

May went home to Utah in the fall of 1947. After several weeks of horseback riding in Logan Canyon and helping her father outdoors, she piled into her brother Roy's car with her parents, and Roy drove them all to see Grace in California. Grace was there trying to break into the movies.

"Hollywood is a curious place," May wrote to Anca on November 12, 1947.

> There is a vivaciousness about the people and the landscape—almost a heedlessness. No one seems ill-humored. There is none of the frenetic feeling of rush, crowding, and aimless speed you find in the East. At the same time you have a feeling of laziness of mind, a disinclination to seriousness. The people irritate me—they are infants politically, that is plain.

May sent this letter to Anca in Czechoslovakia, where she had gone to be reunited with her sister Miriska, who alone of the immediate family had survived the Holocaust. Anca's letters told of her troubles with Miriska, their guilt-filled arguments about their mother. May answered,

> I have the feeling that your sister (perhaps without knowing it herself) really craves to be good to you, to be generous, to give you everything you want. . . . As an experiment, be sweet, gentle, yielding, and see if she will not do a turnabout toward generosity. This sounds like a boring lecture—but it is only my thoughts awkwardly written down. Please take them in that spirit.

In truth, May's friendship with Anca had been difficult, filled with Anca's stormy words about her favorite subjects (politics, economics, and religion) and then falsely smoothed over by May's "lamb-like, resigned, don't-pay-attention-it-will-pass attitude," as May called her own behavior. She had come to believe herself "too humble, smothered, squelched." In New York again after her trip West, she cleaned the Bedford Street apartment, took her books and papers, and moved to a room several blocks away on Perry Street.

May remained a supportive friend of Anca's for a lifetime and left a sum of money to Anca in her will.

Perry Street in Grenwich Village.

Chapter 4

In the Village

23 *Perry Street in the Village.*

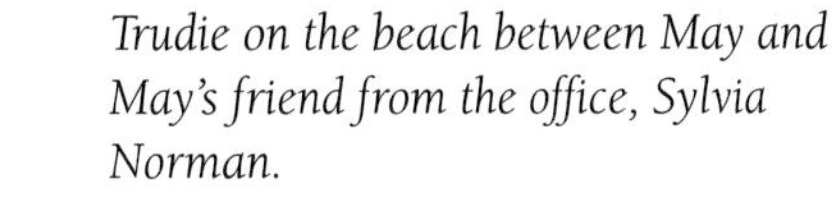

Trudie on the beach between May and May's friend from the office, Sylvia Norman.

May's private room at 23 Perry Street was in a third-floor apartment. There she shared a kitchen and bath with Trudie Lubitsch and another woman, who soon moved out. The empty room became the living room. The apartment had a terrace overlooking a walled-in garden behind St. John's Church. On this terrace she wrote many poems during the next nineteen years.

May's office was in the Federal Wholesale Druggists' Association building on Fifth Avenue. In her eight years there (1942–1949), May worked her way up from typist to editor of two trade publications in the drug industry: *The Federal Pharmacist*,

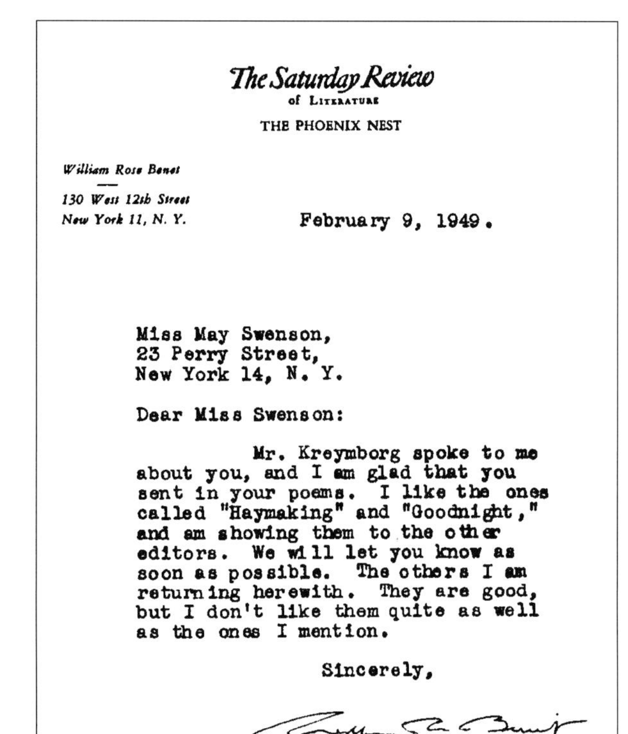
The Saturday Review
of Literature
THE PHOENIX NEST

William Rose Benet
130 West 12th Street
New York 11, N. Y.

February 9, 1949.

Miss May Swenson,
23 Perry Street,
New York 14, N. Y.

Dear Miss Swenson:

Mr. Kreymborg spoke to me about you, and I am glad that you sent in your poems. I like the ones called "Haymaking" and "Goodnight," and am showing them to the other editors. We will let you know as soon as possible. The others I am returning herewith. They are good, but I don't like them quite as well as the ones I mention.

Sincerely,

William Rose Benet

agm

Encs. 3

a monthly, and *The Federal News Capsule*, a weekly. She'd written news releases, letters, and convention speeches for the executive secretary of the association, earning $75 per week by the time she decided to take a year off and live on her savings of $1,000. She wanted to write poems—write and rewrite until they were good enough to attract the attention of sympathetic editors. She planned to tackle the "messy business" of getting to know people who might help her get published.

She already had one influential friend, a fellow Raven Poetry Club member with whom she often played chess: Alfred Kreymborg. A member of the Poetry Society of America and its president from 1943 to 1945, Kreymborg had been a leader in helping poets win recognition, among them Marianne Moore and William Carlos Williams. May invited Kreymborg for tea on January 26, 1949, and asked him to suggest national magazines that might accept her poems. She asked Kreymborg to recommend her to editors. In her diary May wrote:

> Today Kreymborg by the fireplace . . . pushed out his mouth to be kissed. "Don't be afraid," he said and impressed his moist mouth beneath bristled gray on mine. "I wonder what I'm supposed to do about this?" I asked, the remark just a formality because obviously his gentle goatishness doesn't mean anything. . . . He likes my poem "The Stone." But he'd say "Good" about my poetry if I wrote "Shitshitshit."

AN ANNUAL EXHIBITION GALLERY OF NEW & DIVERGENT TRENDS IN MODERN LETTERS

new directions 11

This volume presents a highly varied selection of new writing in the advance guard and experimental fields, both here and abroad. It contains stories, poems, plays and essays by forty-five different writers. There is much here that will arouse controversy and much that will stimulate new lines of thought about literature and open up new areas of appreciation. Some of the highlights are:

- A study of Rimbaud by Henry Miller
- Excerpts from Jean Genet's "Our Lady of Flowers"
- A story and three poems by Tennessee Williams
- An essay on the painter Dove by Duncan Phillips, with reproductions
- A dance play by Kenneth Rexroth
- An essay on the situation of American writers by Stephen Spender
- Poems by contemporary Japanese poets
- A short novel by John Hawkes
- Two stories by the Argentine writer, Jorge Luis Borges
- A new group of poems by W. C. Williams

STORIES by Paul Bowles, Robert Lowry, Lloyd Alexander, H. E. Fenway, Catharine Carver, Allen Chalmers (England), John F. Mathews, Jane Mayhall, Tito Guerrini (Italy), William Burford, Frances Cotton, William Goyen, Audrie Girdner, John Goodwin, Irwin Kroening, and Joseph Shore.

POETRY by Robert Lowry, Peter Viereck, William Burford, Lorine Niedecker, Lynette Roberts (Wales), Willard Maas, Marcia Nardi, Albert Cook, William Jay Smith, Brenda Chamberlain (Wales), Howard Sergeant (England), Sherry Mangan, Harold G. McCurdy, May Swenson, Alain Bosquet (France), Claudio Solar (Chile), Stanley Moss, Edward Field and Edwin Honig.

$4.50

James Laughlin at about the time he first accepted May's poem for New Directions.

May's breakthrough came with the publication of "Haymaking" in *The Saturday Review of Literature* and with a group of poems in *New Directions 11*. May's editor at *New Directions*, James Laughlin, was concerned with publishing controversial, experimental writers. May's poems thus appeared with works by Henry Miller, Jean Genet, Jorge Borges, and other Laughlin favorites.

In the mid 1950s, May began working part-time for Laughlin as a manuscript reader and "chief writer of rejection letters." She held this job for twelve years. "May was such a joy to have around the office, never wasting any time with frivolous chitchat. She was always there if I ever had a serious question about poetry that needed an answer," James Laughlin has written.

We regret that we are unable to use the enclosed material. Thank you for giving us the opportunity to consider it.

THE EDITORS

May received eight letters of rejection from Howard Moss of *The New Yorker* before he phoned to accept "By Morning." Believing that readers would not understand the subject of her poem, he asked May for a title change. She gave in to him only because she wanted to see "Snow by Morning" in the magazine's prestigious pages. It was the first of fifty-nine Swenson poems published there over the next thirty-eight years.

Editors who rejected May's work found it "promising" and "interesting" but also "spoiled by heavy imagery," "too forensic," "too slow," and "lacking in fresh diction." May abandoned many of these poems to the back of a file cabinet. (She never threw poems away!) Others she placed in her "Working" folder for revision. She wrote new poems, put together a collection—*The Green Moment*—and submitted it to the Yale Series of Younger Poets for the prize of publication. The judge was W. H. Auden and May was a finalist but not the winner. Two

THE NEW YORKER
No. 25 WEST 43RD STREET
NEW YORK, 18, N.Y.

VOUCHER NO. 1077
CHECK NO. 3507

3/6/53

TO May Swenson

MS 7227 SNOW BY MORNING

$42.00

DETACH AND DEPOSIT ATTACHED CHECK—RETURN IF INCORRECT

May's first paycheck from The New Yorker.

Howard Moss of The New Yorker *and May at a poetry reading in 1985.*

May was forty years old in this photo taken for the Charles Scribner's Sons publicity file.

other collections—*Sky Acquainted* and *That Never Told Can Be*—made the rounds of publishers only to be sent back with polite notes.

And then! May's fourth collection was accepted by editor John Hall Wheelock for Charles Scribner's Sons on May 28, 1953. He wrote "We have been impressed by the quality and originality of your work as a poet, and I'm glad to be able to report that we should like to publish *Another Animal*. . . . My congratulations to you on the very real achievement this collection of poems represents." May answered "I hope that when I next see you I can tell you what great delight your letter brought—it came on my birthday." Part of May's delight was that Wheelock was a poet himself, and he had worked with Thomas Wolfe on *Of Time and the River*, a novel she had loved.

May's breakthrough into the literary scene included an invitation to Yaddo, a residence and retreat (in Saratoga, New York) for writers, artists, and composers. There in the fall of 1950 May met the poet Elizabeth Bishop and began a long friendship that was conducted mainly by correspondence: May in New York, Elizabeth in Brazil.

Many years after the publication of Another Animal, *May and John Wheelock read his poems to an audience in East Hampton, New York. May helped him from the platform. (Summer, 1975)*

On the grounds of Yaddo, May and Elizabeth Bishop each have an arm around the painter Beauford Delaney, who became May's friend. At his parties in the Village May met James Baldwin, Henry Miller, and others Delaney had painted. Their portraits hung in his studio.

In letters they exchanged opinions about each other's work and plans, sent each other poems for comment, told daily events and bits of gossip.

"Elizabeth's daily life in Brazil is given in fascinating detail with the result that the origins of some of her most famous poems and stories become clear," May wrote when she deposited the letters—her carbons, Elizabeth's originals—in the Special Collections of Washington University in 1984.

May with the artist Nell Blaine and composer John La Montaine at MacDowell Colony, 1957. Nell has written: "May's vision of nature struck a deep chord in me because of her highly developed visual sense."

A before-dinner gathering at Colony Hall, May standing at the fireplace.

Dinner at MacDowell Colony, May facing camera, table at the right.

Hyde Solomon did various charcoal studies of May before completing this oil painting in 1955. May bought two of the studies as well as three of Solomon's later paintings. She also bought paintings and sketches from Rosenquit and Delaney in times when they needed money and May had a bit extra from poetry prizes she had won.

"May Swenson," a painting by Bernard Rosenquit. (June, 1958)

During a later residence at Yaddo, May was a regular at evening seances, helping Ted Hughes and Sylvia Plath "tip the table." May's poem "The Fingers" came from these seances.

May's visual sensitivity was an important link with artists during her frequent stays at Yaddo and at MacDowell Colony in Petersboro, New Hampshire. She played chess with Marcel Duchamp, read poems with Clifford Wright, had sittings for portraits by Beauford Delaney, Hyde Solomon, Bernard Rosenquit, and others.

Colonists at MacDowell sat for a group photo in late summer, 1957. May (far left) is behind poet Louise Bogan. Next to Louise is Milton Avery, who became one of May's favorite artists as she got to know his work well enough to write an article about it for the *1959 Arts Yearbook*. She revered Avery for working independently of schools and movements. She felt a kinship with his lightness of touch, his childlike innocence, his self-deprecating humor, and his concentration on unprepossessing subjects.

Friends of May's that summer (1957) at MacDowell were the composer Ruth Anderson (front row, 4th from left) and Elizabeth Shepley Sergeant (with her hands folded, directly behind Ruth Anderson). May enjoyed Elizabeth's biography of Willa

May's desk in Mixter studio at MacDowell, 1963.

Cather and was helpful and supportive when Elizabeth asked her to read her work-in-progress, a biography of Robert Frost.

May celebrated other favorite artists in her poems: "A Day Like Rousseau's *Dream*," "Picasso: 'Dream,' Oil, 1932" "O'Keeffe Retrospective," "The Tall Figures of Giacometti," and "Angels, Eagles," a poem about the work of Leonard Baskin.

On a scrap of paper on her desk at MacDowell, May scribbled the first line of a future poem: "How long since I slipped into this trough called death?" Also on the desk is an unfinished novel—*A Clean World*—and a folder of new poems May began there in June, 1963: "All that Time," "Gods Children," "Hearing the Wind at Night," "Lighting the Fire," "That One," and "A Yellow Circle."

Also on the desk is a large ashtray. May had been a smoker since her college days, and she was now up to two packs a day—every day. She finally went "cold turkey" in the spring of 1973. She stuck to her resolve without complaint, but later confessed it had taken years to get over completely the urge for a cigarette.

In between stays at MacDowell Colony and Yaddo, May took short-term jobs as a dictaphone operator rather than seek career positions. She wanted mechanical duties with little responsibility in order to save her imagination for poetry in the "left-over edges of each day." She wrote herself this memo:

> Like an animal confined in a narrow, empty, dark, and airless square cage where seemingly the walls, floor, and ceiling are blank and identical, who yet finds with his senses such nourishment as he needs—so I exist in this 8-hour-a-

PETER A. FRASSE AND CO., INC.
Founded 1816

ALLOY, STAINLESS AND COLD FINISHED CARBON STEELS • BARS, TUBES, SHEETS, STRIP AND WIRE

17 GRAND STREET, NEW YORK 13, N.Y.
NEW YORK, WALKER 5-2200 • JERSEY CITY, DELAWARE 3-4888

April 3, 1951

18-A

Kent Tool & Die Inc.
104 South 4th St.
Brooklyn, N.Y.

Subject: OUR 11-N-136796-K5-R

Gentlemen:

Conclusion to Spotted Dress Dream: If every dream contains a hidden wish, what is the wish behind this one? That I wish to outwit and be superior to the saleslady, representing convention, and to persist in being myself, wearing my own personality, etc. But this is not a hidden wish -- I'm very consciously aware of it, and there would be no need for a dream to re-iterate it. The possibility of the opposite -- but that doesn't fit. Possibly the dream points out that there are withim me fragments of the desire to be like others, to conform, and to be approved of by them.

May used office stationery for her dreams in case a supervisor looked over her shoulder.

day confinement where I must turn myself into a mechanism outwardly but can live free inside.

When no one in the office was watching, May typed drafts of poems. She recorded her dreams and analyzed them for a collection she was making, *Chapters of the Night*. She'd taken a course at the New School of Social Research on the interpretation of dreams and had collected a shelf of books on the subject: *How to Understand Your Dreams*, *An Outline of Psychoanalysis*, *An Introduction to Analytic Psychology*, *Art and Artist*, *The Basic Writings of Sigmund Freud*, *The Psychology of*

Women, and eventually many others. These she read for the self-understanding she was always seeking. She took notes to share with close friends who couldn't afford analysis or who were in analysis yet also depended on May's role as a listener and counselor. May herself was too independent, too careful with money to turn to a professional analyst for insight.

"I recently bought Rank's *Will Therapy*," May wrote in a letter to Sylvia Norman. "Rank's insight into the creative personality is particularly rewarding. . . . I like his admission that he, too, is groping up the stairs of life along with his patients and encounters, in the last analysis, only the fog-swept boundaries of the metaphysical."

In book margins May was less complimentary. She wrote "No," "Nuts," "How stupid," "More of the same," "You don't know this," "Ha ha—to him 'sick' means 'different.'" May underlined "What we believed to be true a century ago we know now to be a fallacy."

"Don't forget—this process continues," she added.

THE PREGNANT DREAM

I had a dream in which I had a dream,
and in my dream I told you, "Listen,
I will tell you my dream." And I
began to tell you. And you told me,
"I haven't time to listen while you
tell your dream."

Then in my dream I dreamed I began to
forget my dream. And I forgot my dream.
And I began to tell you, "Listen, I
have forgot my dream." And now I tell
you: "Listen while I tell you my dream,
a dream in which I dreamed I forgot
my dream," and I begin to tell you:
"In my dream you told me, 'I haven't
time to listen.' "

And you tell me: "You dreamed I wouldn't
listen to a dream that you forgot?
I haven't time to listen to forgotten
dreams." "But I haven't forgot I
dreamed," I tell you, "a dream in which
I told you, 'Listen, I have forgot,'
and you told me, 'I haven't time.' "
"I haven't time," you tell me.

And now I begin to forget that I forgot
what I began to tell you in my dream.
And I tell you, "Listen, listen, I
begin to forget."

May at her Perry Street "desk," an old trestle table furnished by her landlord, Father Graf of St. John's Church.

Now May followed a policy of saving part of her salary until she had enough money for months away from the secretarial jobs she held in the 1950s. She would quit jobs to write poems—at her own desk, at writers "colonies," and once at the Bread Loaf Writers' Conference in Vermont. The director, poet John Ciardi, had been impressed with May's book, *Another Animal*, and had named her the Robert Frost Fellow that year. He explained the conference in his letter:

> What it comes to is two weeks of sober talk in the morning and drunken talk thereafter with a widely assorted batch of people from pulp writers on up (or down) who have done some thinking about writing and who manage to say things that can be agreed with or disagreed with profitably.

May accepted Ciardi's offer, not for the social life but because she hoped to connect with an editor for her new collection of poems, *A Cage of Spines*. She also hoped that Frost himself would like her poems and say a word to impress editors.

That didn't happen. "I had a short interview with Frost," May wrote.

> I enjoyed sitting knee-to-knee with him all alone and listening, just absorbing his presence. His specific comment that I remember was that my book "reeks with poetry." He said no more. His handsome old face had an impassive ruffian look. He drew a breath through wide nostrils. His eyes were sharp bits of turquoise. Ponderously he stood up. And I never did find out what he meant. I was too paralyzed to ask.

May stands almost eye to eye with Robert Frost at Bread Loaf, 1957.

A lifelong friend May made that summer was Bread Loaf fellow Alma Routsong. Alma later asked May to read her manuscript *Patience and Sarah*, which was having a tough time finding a publisher. May was entranced with the novel and encouraged Alma never to give up on trying to publish it. The book has since become a classic.

MY MOTHER AND FATHER CAME TO SEE

My mother and father came to see
(clear to New York—
both are over seventy)
me, their daughter. That's Empire State
poking between them. "He's my mate . . ."
Her mouth with dental-plated
smile stretched by patience and the years,
her hand in the print-silk sleeve from Sears,
shy on his arm. They birthed
five boys, five girls (me the first).
My hair, like his, was silversilk.
She let my brothers have her milk
but he made a wooden wheel on a stick
for me, and he let me pick
the biggest of everything because
I was the oldest and I was

May's parents on her terrace at the Perry Street apartment. She showed them the town when they stayed with her on their way to and from their Mormon mission in Sweden (1953-56). Her poem "My Mother and Father Came to See" describes their reactions to a city so unlike their mountain home. Other visitors to Perry Street were brother Roy, also on his way to a Mormon mission in Sweden, sister Grace and her husband, surprising May on their trip from Los Angeles, and Jay Hall, sister Beth's husband traveling to a job in Iran.

a girl. Yes, my dad knew *how*
then. He had a style. And now,

crinkled to the eyebrows that Swedish smile
and blue as bits of ice
(you can feel them even in the black and white) his wise,
small, unperturbed, sunflower seed-shaped peepers:
"Yes, sir. You bet.
She's the best
little wife yet."
Still calls her "Mother." (I used to think it incest.)
Still sleep in the same bed.
Only head
to foot, she told me. On account of?
Well, Martha kissed Jesus' feet.
His toenails porphyry to her, I guess.
He had the whitest skin. Still has,
below the sunburned neck, red
as Arizona stone.
And she never wore
lipstick. Wouldn't hussify herself,
not even to be like Aunt Ruth (blonder, with the pure
soprano: "Ah, Sweet Mystery" could polarize your bones,
turn them to rainbows in your chest;
such a thrill-
ing voice she had; and died of cancer.) Oh,
my mother quick to cry:
do tear ducts fill like breasts
with the same navel tug? I,
the bluish rope never inside me knit,
anymore than sew a round doily for the dresser, with
those fancy nippled knots, haven't ever hardly had
the warm sea in me, saltfresh overflow.

There they sit
on the terrace. (You'd have to say

a "porch" out West.) "A garden's such a blessing
in New York. Close to a miracle." Talking
of rutabagas and how he's sold the bees
now he's half retired and in his seventies.
Still teaching, though, still going to the shop
each day. Those knees
climb College Hill's four hundred steps, cement,
and down again by three
P.M. to water the roses, soak the lawn
(square thumb athwart the nozzle at the groin,
the way he always held it). Powerful stuff,
my father: arched a stream
canyon-cold, sprouting like a dream
of mountain trout;
far as fifty feet he'd throw that fan,
he gushed us good if we came barefoot out
the house in August. Well, it's just the season now

but here the sky is white as semen in raw
egg and, sticky, glazes
the background of their fresh-air faces:
something like a sailor gets, that wind-
scoured skin,
eyes bleached blue,
sharp as pinpoints, prick the horizon
and my conscience, too.
Between them I (and it) look strange,
like if you spent a silver dollar and got change
in a foreign coin: banker's gray,
that slim snout smelling heaven, steel and glass by day,
a big saltshaker of a temple
(pretty impressive, they guess)
or, yes,
a thermometer (rectal) by night,
what with the red-lit tube.

They might look like a rube
to you but they
rode the subway
smart as anybody, and my mother said
the Negroes had
beautiful complexions; she appreciated
that particular purple right away.
And if my father nearly didn't get out
because he waited for all the ladies to go first
through the nervous flop-doors, well,
he isn't dumb, it's his integrity;
and in the lion's den he'd do like Daniel,
yes, he'd charm them just by staying himself.

He's got a powerful lot left, my dad.
My mother, too—if she does cry
every time she reads the paper, how many die
on the highway. There's a portrait
in my mind all about them (not this one
that doesn't fit—with the silly lead paperweight
in the middle): their heads with a
squareness like a good bull
and cow, bred
for stubbornness, stamina, no
nonsense, and lots of heart. Or going the whole
hog (I don't mind), like ears of corn,
solid, full-grown, husky, yet
tender as buttercups: that's my ma and pa, going
away now, reverse closeup, riding west

away from the camera. Together,
like on a medallion, dignified, or on a crested
shield of blue. Skating to bluer blue, to the real
sky out there that they made blue
and the yellow sun. Getting small now but bigger

May with her parents in Logan. (November, 1959)

in a sort of way as if they'd
always be there. They will, too.
(Those heads are three dimensional.) To "where
you really belong" and long—"It's been so long."
And long to but won't be, can't be,
being the stubbornest
(and too tall
between them), being the first
and oldest, after all.

The first time May's parents heard her read her poems publicly was at the college in Logan in 1959. Her second book, *A Cage of Spines*, had been published that year, a result of her efforts at the Bread Loaf conference, and May was on a reading tour. For this homecoming, May's mother planned a family gathering that included all of May's twenty-three nieces and nephews. In a letter to a friend, May wrote:

> My home college in Logan gave me quite a welcome, and I, surprisingly, enjoyed reading for a large group. (I had dreaded it!) A favorite professor of mine,

Dr. Pederson, now eighty years old, introduced me. It was a new and peculiar experience being a so-called "celebrity" and hailed in the newspaper and all.

May also gave readings in San Francisco and Berkeley—a reading circuit organized by Betty Kray, director of the Poetry Center in New York. Betty Kray encouraged May to travel to college campuses and read her poetry as a way to supplement her meager income. May's first reading had been at the Center after a group of her poems

The Poetry Center 1955-56

John Malcolm Brinnin, Consultant
M. J. Brodney (Mrs.), Secretary

Subscriptions - - $15.00
Single Admission - 2.00

TWENTY OR MORE EVENINGS AT 8:40

TENNESSEE WILLIAMS Sunday, October 16
Reading scenes from "Camino Real" with **ELI WALLACH**

ELIZABETH BOWEN Saturday, October 22
speaking on "Writing a Novel"

MARIANNE MOORE Saturday, October 29
speaking on "Words and Modes of Expression"

W. H. AUDEN Saturday, November 5

TRUMAN CAPOTE Sunday, November 20

e. e. cummings Saturday, December 3

*** FINNEGAN'S WAKE** Saturday, December 10
a dramatization-demonstration of James Joyce's novel by the Poets Theatre of Cambridge, Mass. "Finnegan's Wake is an old story. All the old stories. The oldest in the world—love, death, joy, hatred, suspicion, ribaldry, faith, sacrifice, heroism, redemption and rebirth—as they are experienced by every condition of man in every age and climate, to man's own never-ceasing astonishment."
—John V. Kelleher

ARCHIBALD MACLEISH Saturday, December 17

ANTHONY HECHT and ALISTAIR REID Wednesday, January 11

DELMORE SCHWARTZ and MAY SWENSON Wednesday, January 25

**** VALERIE BETTIS AND DANCE COMPANY** Sunday, January 29
Featuring William Faulkner's "As I Lay Dying" and John Malcolm Brinnin's "Desperate Heart" and other works.

KATHERINE ANNE PORTER Wednesday, February 1

EDWIN MUIR Sunday, February 12

MARY MC CARTHY Wednesday, February 15

RUSSELL OBERLIN Sunday, February 26
singing Elizabethan love songs with harpsichord accompaniment.

JOHN MALCOLM BRINNIN and RICHARD WILBUR Wednesday, March 7

LOUISE BOGAN and MAY SARTON Wednesday, March 14

ROBERT FROST Sunday, March 25

PETER KANE DUFALT and JAMES MERRILL Wednesday, April 4

ARTHUR MILLER Date to be announced

MOSS HART Date to be announced

* Also Sunday, December 11 at 3:00 p.m. (Not on series)
** Also Sunday, January 29 at 3:00 p.m. (Not on series)

Signing her latest book after a reading at Smith College, May looks grimly businesslike. She was nervous when reading and afterward uncomfortable at playing the celebrity.

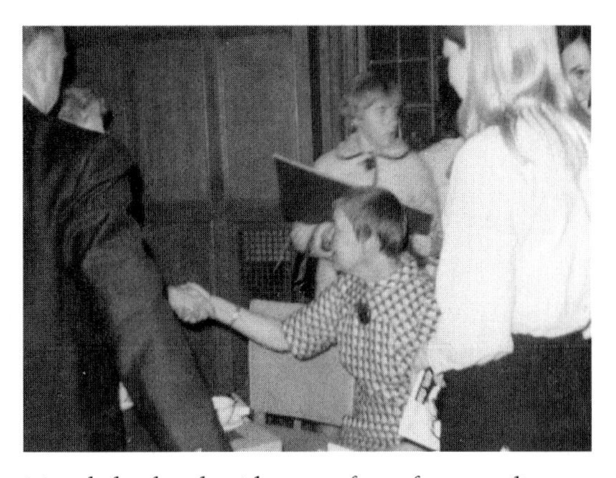

May shakes hands with poetry fans after a reading at Purdue University (Spring 1967). By this time she owned a tape recorder, which she used while practicing each poem over and over. Nonetheless, she never lost her nervousness, only learned to hide it somewhat.

had won the Center's Introduction Prize of $200.00. The judges were Mark Van Doren, John Malcolm Brinnin, and Jean Garrigue.

Traveling with May to readings was her housemate from Perry Street, Pearl Schwartz. May called her "Blackie." They had met in the spring of 1949, and Pearl moved in with May a year later. Trudie Lubitsch remained, so the rent was split three ways, a boost for them all. Pearl worked as a hospital attendant, helping to support her mother, who lived nearby in Brooklyn. Her father had deserted the family—Pearl and two brothers—years earlier.

May described Pearl (in a letter) as "vivid, intelligent, generous, kind, sensitive—a beautiful person." She encouraged Pearl to finish her schooling at Hunter College and find a job that was passionately satisfying. Pearl eventually became a social worker. She was well liked by May's friends. An avid reader and fine writer herself, Pearl fit right in with the people May had met at various writers' retreats, readings, publishing houses, and other literary gatherings.

May was able to give up her poetry readings and also take a leave from her job at New Directions when she won both a Guggenheim Foundation grant and an Amy Lowell Traveling Scholarship. She wrote her mother: "Mom, you must be praying

photo: Fred W. McDarrah

May read her poems at the Nicholas Cafe on the Bowery in 1959, the end of the "Beat Decade." She was not in the clique of Beat poets in New York, but she sometimes shared the stage with them. She also shared their beliefs in the unimportance of money and social position. Her own revolt against consumerism is evident in all she did.

Pearl Schwartz at Jones Beach.

May (left) with Pearl (hatless) and writer friends on a rock at Wildwood, Long Island.

Jane Mayhall, Leslie Katz, and Pearl Schwartz watching for birds. The Katzes were May's friends from her first stay at Yaddo and later stays at the Katz's summer house—Grandstand—in Saratoga. May's poem "Shift of Scene at Grandstand" describes a meadow walk with its "spry chickadees" and "spangle-skirted" rain.

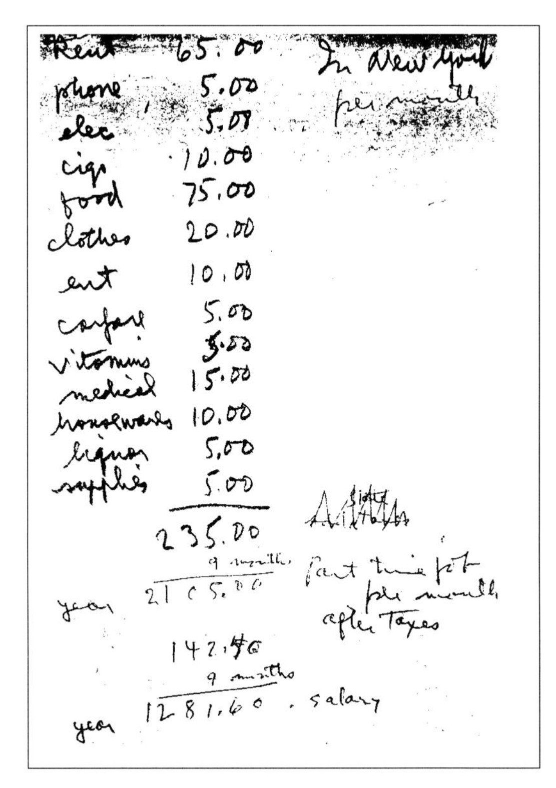

Rent	65.00	In New York per month
phone	5.00	
elec	5.00	
cigs	10.00	
food	75.00	
clothes	20.00	
ent	10.00	
carfare	5.00	
vitamins	5.00	
medical	15.00	
housewares	10.00	
liquor	5.00	
supplies	5.00	
	235.00	
	9 months	
year	2115.00	
	142.40	Part time job per month after taxes
	9 months	
year	1281.60	salary

For her 1959 Guggenheim application, May figured out her monthly living expenses and the yearly salary she made from her part-time job at New Directions.

extra hard for me." With Pearl, May decided to see as much of France, Spain, and Italy as she could in a year (1960). To stretch their funds they bought cooking gear, sleeping bags, a tent, and a French car in order to spend many nights in camps, where such delights as great umbrella pines and gray-white long-horned cows seemed to impress May as much as did the museums, cathedrals, and ancient ruins on the picture postcards she bought to use as a trip diary. Her poems of this time show her appreciation for the natural wonders of Europe.

May's first car, a Simca, parked under the pines of Italy. Pearl did the driving. May had never learned to drive and didn't in Europe, despite Pearl's lessons.

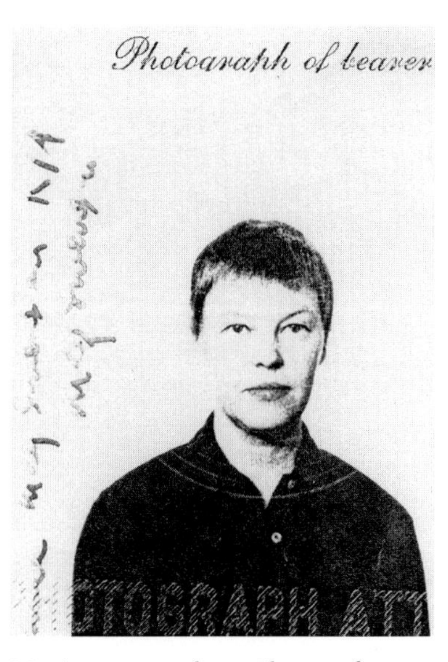

May's passport photo. She was forty-seven years old.

ITALIAN SAMPLER

Lombardy, Tuscany, Umbria, Calabria.
A spear of leaves. A pear.
A clod-filled pasture dark as a bear.
Yellow blazes around a crown.

Lombardy, Tuscany, Umbria, Calabria.
Somber oxen. September flares.
Wind and silk, parchment and candles.
Slumberous, plushy, ponderous, elaborate.

A tree, a fruit, a pigment, an ornament.
Plumes, juices, bristles, crystals.
A mast. A horn. A bramble. A bride.
Lombardy, Tuscany, Umbria, Calabria.

Pearl at one of Rome's many fountains, used by May in her poem "Fountains of Aix."

Back home in the Village, May and Pearl garaged the Simca during winters, then used it for camping vacations in summers. Over the years they had become ardent bird watchers, and the car helped them build up their life lists of birds. In 1961, they camped at Wildwood, Long Island, with Margaret Marshall, the poetry editor of The Nation *for many years.*

May never learned to swim even though friends tried to teach her. Here Ruth Anderson gives her a lesson in the Mediterranean, off shore from Cannes. Ruth was then living in Paris, studying composition with Nadia Boulanger.

Breakfast at a Tom's River campsite in New Jersey.

For the Swenson family photo of August 26, 1962, May stands in the 2nd row from the top, 5th from right. She thought of her poems as her children and was unashamed of having no children in this crowd.

In the summer of 1962, May's parents celebrated their fiftieth wedding anniversary. May's gift was a prosy poem and a $1,000.00 bill, money she'd saved from sales of her poems, including the advance on her third collection, *To Mix With Time,* published by Scribner's in 1963.

That was the year her father died. May's sister Margaret has written this account of his stroke:

> Dad had come in from working in the garden. He ate lunch and sat down in the chair May had given him. My mother noticed he was trying to say something but couldn't speak. As my sister Ruth knelt by Dad's chair he took hold of her hand and began rubbing it along his leg while repeating the words "Feel me to do right." May flew home from New York, and Ruth told her about the strange words Dad had spoken. These led to her wonderful poem called "Feel Me." It is a blessing to me every time I read it.

FEEL ME

"Feel me to do right," our father said on his deathbed.
We did not quite know—in fact, not at all—what he meant.
His last whisper was spent as through a slot in a wall.
He left us a key, but how did it fit? "Feel me
to do right." Did it mean that, though he died, he would be felt
through some aperture, or by some unseen instrument
our dad just then had come to know? So, to do right always,
we need but feel his spirit? Or was it merely his apology
for dying? "Feel that I do right in not trying,
as you insist, to stay on your side. There is the wide
gateway and the splendid tower, and you implore me
to wait here, with the worms!"

Had he defined his terms, and could we discriminate
among his motives, we might have found out how to "do right"
before *we* died—supposing he felt he suddenly knew
what dying was. "You do wrong because you do not feel
as I do now," was maybe the sense. "Feel me, and emulate
my state, for I am becoming less dense—I am feeling right
for the first time." And then the vessel burst,
and we were kneeling around an emptiness.

We cannot feel our father now. His power courses through us,
yes, but *he*—the chest and cheek, the foot and palm,
the mouth of oracle—is calm. And we still seek
his meaning. "*Feel* me," he said, and emphasized that word.
Should we have heard it as a plea for a caress—
a constant caress, since flesh to flesh was all that we
could do right if we would bless him?
The dying must feel the pressure of that question—
lying flat, turning cold from brow to heel—the hot
cowards there above protesting their love, and saying,
"What can we do? Are you all right?" While the wall opens
and the blue night pours through. "What can we do?
We want to do what's right."

"Lie down with me, and hold me, tight. Touch me. Be
with me. Feel with me. *Feel* me to do right."

May left "Feel Me" unfinished, unpublished (until 1968). She was diverted from this and other poems by a theatre-associates grant from the Ford Foundation, which pointed her back to writing plays. She had written comic dramas for her newspaper column at college, and in the late 1930s, she'd tossed off a comedy about the problems of people on relief. Now she dug in and read plays for a year. (Her favorites were by Samuel Becket and Eugene Ionesco.) She attended rehearsals of "The Changeling" at Lincoln Center to learn stagecraft from director Elia Kazan, then wrote draft after draft of her own play, "The Floor," accepting suggestions from the cast and director before opening night.

"The Floor" was given eighteen performances. May thought of it as a comedy of the absurd based on the underlying notion that people are forced by time to live in one dimension—on the floor. "Time confines," she wrote. "Space gives it limits."

My character Hobob has the conviction that there are other dimensions. He intuits the cube, but his life is on one plane. If it were not for time, death's border, man could live in Space, an infinite dimension, his potentiality utilized without limit.

The New York Times.

SUNDAY, MAY 8, 1966.

NYT Pictures

"DOUBLES AND OPPOSITES"—Andrew Glaze and May Swenson, both poets, and Bruce Jay Friedman, author of the novel "A Mother's Kisses," now venture into playwriting, "Doubles and Opposites" will comprise a triple bill of "The Floor" by Miss Swenson, "23 Pat O'Brien Movies" by Friedman and "Miss Pete" by Glaze. They are to open to American Place Theater audiences on Wednesday night.

A theatre-associate grant from the Ford Foundation in 1965 gave May time free of her job for writing a play.

Chapter 5

A Purdue Interlude

For the academic year 1966-67, May accepted an appointment as writer-in-residence at Purdue University in Lafayette, Indiana. She taught English 507, The Writing of Poetry, even though she believed steadfastly that poetry writing was a process that could not be taught. Moreover, May was, in her own words, "scared to death" to get up in front of a class. In the past, she had turned down several offers to teach in colleges closer to New York.

May on her way to her office in the English department at Purdue University

But she could not turn down $20,000.00 for the light duties of teaching twelve students once a week in a three-hour seminar. May reasoned that if she led her usual frugal life in Indiana, she could save much of her salary to live on in the future.

May leveled with her students. On her first day in the classroom she read from prepared notes:

> I don't consider myself a teacher. I do profess my belief in poetry. All my work is experimental and when I begin a poem I don't know what it's going to turn into specifically. I don't start out with form or a rigid plan or any kind of pattern. I have never studied prosody nor have I ever deliberately tried to write a formal poem. Nor have I ever studied under another poet or enrolled in a class or workshop in poetry. I can't teach anyone how to write poetry but I can try to teach why the writing of poetry can't be taught.

May's lack of ease with teaching sometimes led to migraine headaches. Rather than walk back to her own apartment in such pain, she took refuge at a friend's house on campus.

Members of the English department took May on excursions around Indiana. She especially liked the farms on the outskirts of Lafayette with their horses, hogs, and many species of birds.

May wrote careful lesson plans. For example, for one session she asked her students to bring favorite poems for discussion that led into a lecture on how to avoid imitation:

> The reason a good diet of other poets' poems is helpful is that such a diet adds richness to the soil your seed grows in. You are the loam of your poems—your character, personality, experience, and sensitivity, your wishes, griefs, loves, frustrations, and searchings into what life is all about. How you feel and how you give form to your feelings in a poem is more important than how anyone else has ever done it.

Rozanne—called "Zan"—Knudson, a fellow faculty member at Purdue, has written:

> Members of the English department had been gossiping about driving May to the grocery store. I volunteered in order to meet a famous poet. At first, May and I had little in common besides our love for poetry. My spare time was taken up with sports—playing squash several hours a day and watching Purdue's

May had always wanted a driver's license. Here she tries out a VW owned by Zan, who concluded after dozens of lessons that May's poor depth perception (she was near-sighted) was a main cause of her failure to pass the licensing test.

May and Zan on the Purdue University campus.

Al's bar was across town, out of sight of professors, most of whom May found rigid in their tastes, and stuffy. Al's jukebox played soul and gospel; the customers ate barbeque.

May recording sounds on her reel-to-reel.

May's disappointment with the dowdy dust jackets for her first books prompted her to offer suggestions to Scribner's designers for her fifth book, Half Sun Half Sleep, *published while May was at Purdue.*

teams. May knew nothing about sports, but was willing to attend games with me. In return, I agreed to go with her on a birdwalk along the railroad tracks that ran near the small apartment she was renting on Grant Street. That day she pointed out the chipping sparrow, then showed it to me in a guide to North American birds. I was hooked by the 700 or so other North American species that I could eventually add to my life list.

May won two grants while she lived on Grant Street.

Composing sound pieces on her reel-to-reel tape recorder was May's hobby while living in Indiana. She used raw sounds she made by rolling marbles in a pan, for example, or spinning coins on counter tops, swinging squeaking doors, blowing whistles she had collected, and pumping up her air mattress with a noisy pump. She altered these sounds by playing them at many speeds on the tape recorder. Then she arranged the sounds into pieces: "Squeaks and Doodles," "Harsh Assortment," "Strange Love," and "Mechanical Animals," among others. She sometimes sent these to Ruth Anderson for comment. Ruth was by then teaching at Hunter College in New York, working with students in a sound laboratory. May collected tapes of Ruth's compositions and LP records of electronic music by Edgar Varèse, Otto Luening, Vladimir Ussachevsky, and other composers.

ELECTRONIC SOUND

A pebble swells to a boulder at low speed.
At 7½ *ips* a hiss is a hurricane.
The basin drain
is Charybdis sucking
a clipper down, the ship
a paperclip
whirling. Or gargle, brush your teeth, hear
a winded horse's esophagus lurch
on playback at 15/16. Perch
a quarter on edge on a plate, spin:
a locomotive's wheel is wrenched loose,
wobbles down the line to slam the caboose,
keeps on snicking over the ties
till it teeters on the embankment,
bowls down a cement
ramp, meanders onto the turnpike
and into a junkhole
of scrapped cars. Ceasing to roll,
it shimmies, falters . . .
sudden inertia causes
pause.
Then a round of echoes
descending, a minor yammer
as when a triangle's nicked by the slimmest hammer.

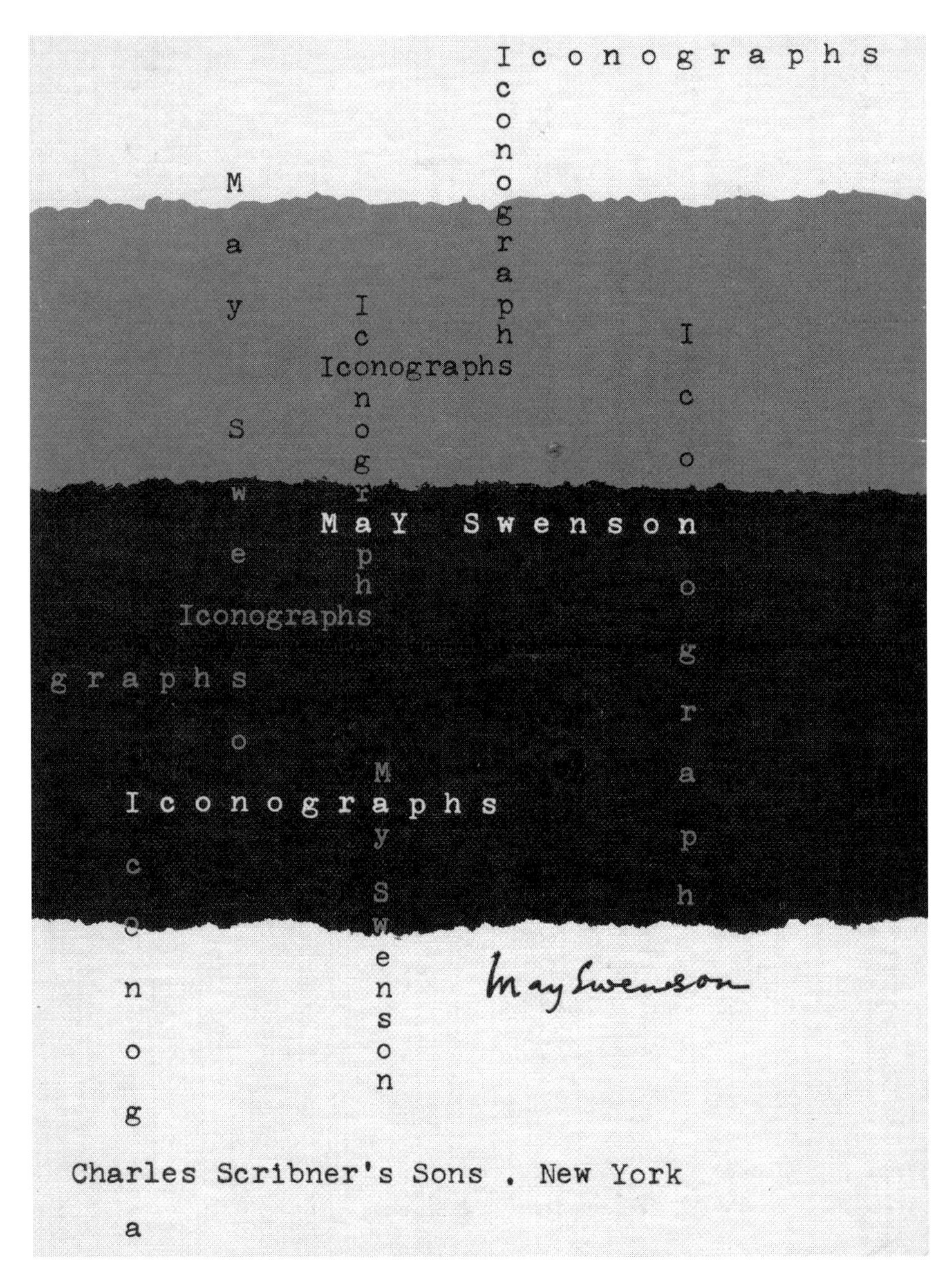

Scribner's allowed May to design her own cover for Iconographs, *a collection of her shape poems. Some of these take place in Indiana, among them "The Power House," a building just steps away from her Grant Street apartment.*

The
POWER
HOUSE

Close to my
place is the
power house.
I knew there
wouldn't be
anybody in it.
It's beauti-
ful. Like a
church. It
works all by
itself. And
with almost no
sound. All glass.
And a tall square
tower on it.
Colored lights
shine from within.
They color the
glass. Pink. Pale
green. Not stained.
Not that kind. And
not fragile. Just
light. Light weight.
A red rod erect
from the tower
blinking on top red. Behind it gray wings of motion. A fan
of light opening and folding somewhere in the west of town.
Periodic as a metronome.
The crickets were talking electricity. A white Spitz barked
at me though my sneakers made no noise. I walked up the
slight slope-- it's wide-- to the power house. Went past
the doorway. Big as a barn door squared. Big horse I thought.
I saw through the doorway gray metal coils. All the clean
machinery and engines. I don't know what to call it all. I
don't know the names.
Painted pretty colors slick and clean. I knew there
wouldn't be anybody there. Nobody needs to work there
I thought. And walked past that door farther on.
White lights icy and clean. Not blazing. Cool.
Gossamer. The pink and green like-sherbet-colors bathing the gray machines.
Came to a place where vapor cooled my skin. A breeze made by waterspray
up high. And there was white steam unfurling
evaporating against the dark.
Down lower a red transparent ball on a pedestal. Incandescent. Big. A
balloon mystery. Inside through another doorway I saw a hook painted
yellow. Huge and high enough to lift a freight car.
I stood looking in-- my shadow so long and black
from the streaming lights.
And I was wrong. Somebody moved in the powerhouse.
Came from between the coils and giant tubes.
Down off the balcony on the steel stairway smooth
and slow. Like floating. Like not having to
look or think. I thought he'd be a Negro but he
wasn't. He didn't see me. Didn't need to see
anything. He had a red face and a blue uniform.

Chapter 6

Sea Cliff, Long Island

At the turn of the century, summer visitors to Sea Cliff landed at the steamship pier and rode uphill in horse-drawn carriages.

In the fall of 1967, May and Zan bought a cedar summer cottage on the North Shore of Long Island in the village of Sea Cliff. Their address for the next twenty-two years was 73 The Boulevard, a street that borders the sands of Long Island Sound. In earlier years, The Boulevard had been called Shore Road.

The present-day village of Sea Cliff dates from the 1870s, when Methodist camp meetings were held on this cliff above the Sound. Worshipers from New York City,

Many of Sea Cliff's carpenter Gothic houses are pictured here. May took a daily walk on the beach along The Boulevard, and up the hill to Sea Cliff's library and post office.

This scene was ever-changing from the window above May's desk. Here a yacht has washed up after a storm. On the far shore, across Long Island Sound, is Larchmont and Mamaroneck in Westchester County.

During May's first winter in Sea Cliff, the Sound froze almost as far west as Westchester County. Ice was thick enough for walking hundreds of yards from shore. This cold weather killed much of the vegetation in the terraces at 73 The Boulevard.

It wasn't long before May's terrace became a stop-off for a family of raccoons. In years to come they fed on table scraps and dog biscuits during all but the coldest months, when they hibernated in a den under the terrace.

twenty-five miles away, came by train or by steamboat to a pier off Sea Cliff Beach. Later the village became a haven for crowds escaping the city's heat. Hotels were built, then summer cottages, and eventually year-round houses for the many writers, painters, photographers, musicians, theatre people, and others who settled in this one-mile square community.

May named the house "Kestrel's Nest" after a species of hawk seen perched on telephone wires across Hempstead Harbor from The Boulevard.

The Kestrel's Nest years later. Forty steps had to be climbed from The Boulevard to the house.

May in the galley-sized kitchen. She never complained about doing dishes but left most of the other housework to Zan, who enjoyed doing it for the exercise.

May and Zan had bought the house furnished. A sectional couch nearly filled the living room, leaving little space for May's desk. They decided to put a "for sale" ad in the local newspaper. May wrote one that made the couch sound like it had fallen out of heaven! Yet, despite her poet's words, the couch didn't find a buyer, so Zan carried all five sections down the forty steps to the beach parking lot, from which they were quickly stolen. The same fate befell almost all the original furniture.

A daily visitor to 73 The Boulevard was Robert Van Vorst, the mailman. Mail was very life to May, bringing answers to her "letters to the world." Having the same friendly and reliable mailman for twenty years was a boon.

At the Van Vorst's Christmas parties May could sit back and enjoy the talented family singing carols.

The writers Alice Geffen, left, and Carole Bergle, center, with Susan Avery, a bookstore owner, on the 4th of July, 1976—Tall Ships Day in New York.

May and Zan gave an annual 4th of July party on their terrace for Sea Cliff friends who wanted a ringside seat for the fireworks display on the beach. For America's bicentennial celebration in 1976, friends came to see the tall ship *Winston Churchill* moored near the Sea Cliff Yacht Club.

JULY 4TH

Gradual bud and bloom and seedfall speeded up
are these mute explosions in slow motion.

From vertical shoots above the sea, the fire
flowers open, shedding their petals.

Black waves, turned more than moonwhite, pink
ice, lightning blue, echo our gasps of admiration

as they crash and hush. Another bush ablaze
snicks straight up. A gap like heartstop between

the last vanished particle and the thuggish boom.
And the thuggish boom repeats in stutters

from sandhill hollows in the shore. We want
more. A twirling sun, or dismembered chrysanthemum

bulleted up, leisurely bursts, in an instant
timestreak is suckswooped back to its core.

And we want more: we want red giant, white dwarf,
black hole, extinct, orgasmic, all in one!

"I get bored with the conventional stanza-and-verse look of poetry. Varying the typography can add a pleasure," May wrote to explain the shape poems in *Iconographs*, her first book published after she moved to Sea Cliff. "I wanted to make my poems do what they say. For example, when you look at 'How Everything Happens' you see just six lines, each a sentence and each one acts typographically according to what it is saying. It climbs or it descends or it lies straight and flat. The spaces between the lines are actively and visually important, too."

May wrote twenty or so water-watching poems during her first years in Sea Cliff. After all, she saw Long Island Sound *from* every room in the house.

She saw sports *in* every room, for Zan's TVs were tuned to games on weekends. May preferred to watch with the sound turned off. This way, she could make up her own versions of the games, as she did in her poem "Watching the Jets Lose to Buffalo at Shea," (see page 147). She wrote "Analysis of Baseball" after attending a game at Yankee Stadium—her first and only live baseball game.

HOW EVERYTHING HAPPENS

(Based on a Study of the Wave)

happen.
to
up
stacking
is
something
When nothing is happening

When it happens
something
pulls
back
not
to
happen.

When has happened.
pulling back stacking up
happens

has happened stacks up.
When it something nothing
pulls back while

Then nothing is happening.

happens.
and
forward
pushes
up
stacks
something
Then

The Washington Post

AN INDEPENDENT NEWSPAPER

'The Ball, the Bat, and the Mitt'

THE SERIES was supposed to be over after game two when, in the flush of a "mighty Casey" melodrama, the young Dodger pitcher, Bob Welch, struck out the mighty, if preposterous, Reggie Jackson to end the ninth. Instead, what happened from that point on was that the Series became a sequence of mere baseball games, and in that sequence we saw what the sport is made of. The Yankees prevailed because they hit more singles, made fewer errors, moved more men around the bases, pitched steadier and, thanks to Graig Nettles, changed the meaning of playing third base. Except for Mr. Nettles, there was nothing spectacular about their performance; but it was relentless.

Relentlessness is exactly what the Dodgers didn't have. They relented after squawking about Mr. Jackson's base-running antics in game four; and they kept on relenting into inning nine, game six, as they watched Goose Gossage—looking both detached and driven—throw the ball past them. When Steve Garvey took a third strike for the next to last out, only Dodger manager Tommy Lasorda showed a glimmer of hope, and that was half ritualistic. In their dugout the Yankees rocked back and forth, chewed, clapped and anticipated champagne.

They had come into this 75th World Series as the Pittsburgh Pirates had come into the first—their third straight pennant; a strong, balanced team hampered by injuries. The difference was that in 1903 the Pirates lost to the Boston Pilgrims, whereas the Yankees were not to be denied. They won it playing hurt, and coming back. They won it at the bottom of the batting order. And they won it with small heroes—Bucky Dent and Brian Doyle—who proved that the game is still played in simple acts. Even the garish championship trophy presented by Commissioner Bowie Kuhn, which looked like a church designed by Dolly Parton, couldn't damage the proceedings.

One of the odd things about this Series is that neither the Yankee comeback nor the Dodger collapse ever seemed unthinkable. Professionalism isn't always a virtue, but it was for the Yankees, who not once gave the impression that they expected to lose. Of course, that's easier said in retrospect, where theories abound. For now, let it be said simply that the Yanks played baseball as the poet, May Swenson has cleanly understood the game: "It's about / the ball, / the bat, / and the mitt."

An editorial from the Washington Post used a line from May's "Analysis of Baseball" for its headline, and then noted that May has "cleanly understood the game." Reprinted by permission of The Washington Post.

The Swedish poet Thomas Tranströmer (left) with May and the linguist Leif Sjoberg at a reading from Windows & Stones, *May's translations of Tranströmer's poems.*

As a child May spoke only Swedish (until she entered first grade) and she retained some facility with the language all her life. In the 1960s the Bollingen Foundation had sponsored her translations of the Swedish poets Ingemar Gustafson, Werner Aspenström, Eric Lindegren, Gunnar Ekelöf, Harry Martinson, and Karin Boye; and May had included them in her collection *Half Sun Half Sleep*. Now in 1970 she was asked by the University of Pittsburgh Press to translate poems by the noted Swedish poet Thomas Tranströmer for a collection to be published by the Press. For this May worked closely with the linguist Leif Sjoberg but still claimed she made some "funny errors" and "went off the track" in certain poems! She found Tranströmer's work "searching, honest, direct, natural, and unforced" with "unexpected reverberations and afterimages." For May, translating was like "solving puzzles—absorbing, difficult but satisfying when it seems I hit something right."

May's poems about science were gaining attention. Their inclusion in such anthologies as *Science and the Human Spirit* placed May on pages with Isaac Newton, J. Robert Oppenheimer, and James D. Watson. She relished the association. She relished also her new

SWENSON, May, poet; b. **Logan, Utah,** May 28. 1919; d. Dan Arthur and **Margaret (Helborg)** S.; B.S., Utah State U., 1939. Poet in residence Purdue U., Lafayette, Ind., 1966-67. Author: (poems) Another Animal, 1954; A Cage of Spines, 1958; To Mix With Time, 1963; Poems to Solve, 1966; Half Sun Half Sleep, 1967. Recipient Nat. Inst. Arts and Letters award, 1960, Brandeis U. award, 1967, Shelley Meml. award Poetry Soc. Am., 1968; Guggenheim fellow, 1959; Amy Lowell Travelling scholar, 1960; Ford Found. fellow, 1965; Rockefeller Found. fellow, 1967-68, Lucy Martin Donnally fellow Bryn Mawr Coll., 1968-69. Home: 73 Boulevard, Sea Cliff. N.Y. 11579.

In 1970, May's name was added to Who's Who in America. *She showed her pride by buying a copy of that huge, heavy book for her library.*

May at the space museum at Cape Canaveral. She also spent several days at the National Air and Space Museum in Washington D.C. At home, she religiously followed newspaper and TV accounts of America's space program, and in 1984 she watched a launching of the space shuttle from a campsite a mile directly inland from the launch pad.

CEREMONIAL PROGRAM

Opening of the Ceremonial by the President of the Academy — GEORGE F. KENNAN

Induction of New Academy Members by the President of the Academy

ELLIOTT C. CARTER JOSÉ DE CREEFT
RAPHAEL SOYER

Induction of New Institute Members by the Secretary of the Institute — BABETTE DEUTSCH

DEPARTMENT OF ART

JOHN KOCH ROBERT MOTHERWELL
ROBERT LAURENT* KEVIN ROCHE

DEPARTMENT OF LITERATURE

CLEANTH BROOKS PHILIP ROTH
ANTHONY HECHT JEAN STAFFORD
DWIGHT MACDONALD MAY SWENSON
JOSEPH MITCHELL C. VANN WOODWARD
WRIGHT MORRIS

DEPARTMENT OF MUSIC

DUKE ELLINGTON NICOLAS NABOKOV

*died April 20, 1970

membership in the National Institute of Arts and Letters. She was delighted to write to her mother: "You may not remember a pair of lace stockings you sent me long ago. Well, I'm going to wear them with a yellow lace dress to the ceremonial at the National Institute where I'm to be inaugurated next Tuesday."

May's mother answered, "Congratulations for the great honors that come to you because of that wonderful gift of yours as a poet, a gift no doubt inherited from your father and grandfather who were both writers, as you know."

May's mother, Margaret Hellberg Swenson, died in June, 1972. May flew to Logan to speak at the funeral and later that summer she returned to Utah by car to get her father's prize-winning cellarette, left to May in her mother's will. Then, for the month of August, May lived in her mother's house and taught a poetry workshop at Utah State University. The comfort of being near her Logan brother Dan and sister Ruth and among old college friends helped May face the loss of her mother.

Although May never came to feel comfortable in front of a group, she accepted short teaching stints in the 1970s at the University of Lethbridge in Canada, at the University of California–Riverside, and at the University of North Carolina–Greensboro, and at several public schools in New York. She scheduled her teaching jobs and her readings to fit in with the camping trips she loved taking to national forests, parks, and monuments. Zan did the driving. She liked best visiting sites where writers had once lived and worked.

"The teachers and students treated me like a celebrity," May wrote after teaching and reading for four days in Wappingers Falls, New York.

Joshua Tree National Monument.

May at D.H. Lawrence's ranch near Taos, New Mexico.

At the Circle "Z" ranch in Arizona, May went trail riding with the other dudes while Zan searched for the common black-hawk and the five-striped sparrow.

Red Cloud, Nebraska, the center of Catherland, was a short detour from main highways leading west. May is standing with one of the many Willa Cather markers in Webster County.

Susan Yankowitz reads at the Women's Salon in New York. May at right.

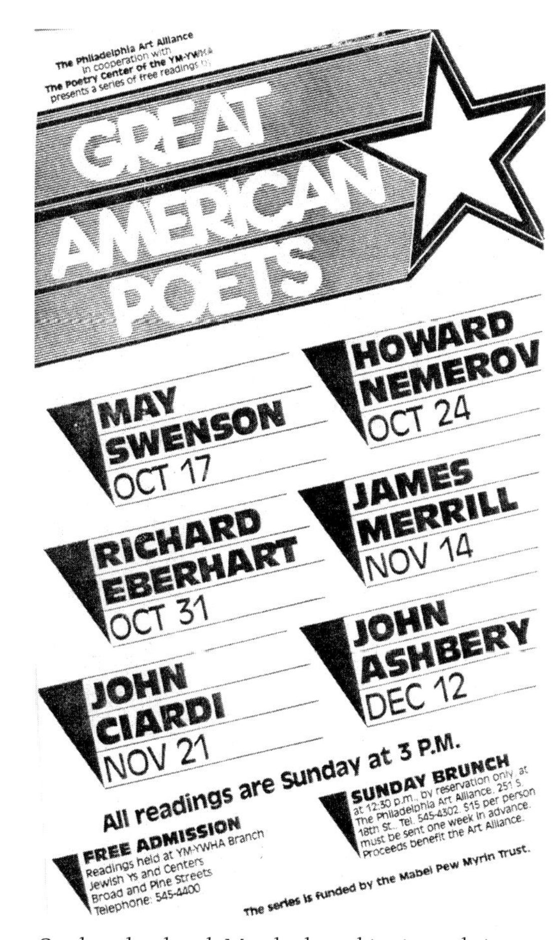

On the other hand, May had no objection to being called a "great American poet"!

> I don't think there is a feminine poetic consciousness—nor is there a masculine one. I even hate the designation 'woman poet.' How silly it would sound to say 'man poet.'

May wrote these words to an anthologist who wanted to put her poems in a women-only collection. May agreed to contribute, but she nonetheless hoped to change the anthologist's mind about the restrictive collection. And May usually refused readings to women-only audiences. She made an exception when asked to join her friend Susan Yankowitz at the Women's Salon in New York City.

In 1973, May and Zan began spending winters away from their poorly heated cottage in Sea Cliff. May had a nasal allergy that brought on asthma attacks, and these were less troublesome in warm climates. For two winters, they lived in Arizona and came to know the desert. For three winters, they had an apartment across the street from UCLA's botanical gardens in Westwood, Los Angeles. There May could walk to her heart's content. Other favorite walks were a path under the coral trees in Santa Monica and along the oceanfront sidewalk at Venice Beach.

May with the poets Jean Burden (center) and Ann Stanford at a party given by Ann at her home in Beverly Hills (1978). May and Ann admired each other's poetry and became good friends in California.

May on a day when there were no runners to dodge on San Vicente Boulevard in Los Angeles.

On trips along the California coast in search of birds, May liked to sample whatever crops were growing near the road. Here, artichokes.

A stay at Dorland Mountain Colony in Temecula, California, gave May hundreds of acres to roam in search of lines for poems. "Last night coyotes bayed nearby in weird harmony," May wrote in her prose poem about Dorland, "Rainbow Hummingbird Lamplight."

> . . . Across the gulch, sharing the top twigs of a wrung-dry dead yucca with fierce thrasher and pushy jay—what a sweet surprise—was Anna's hummingbird. Only a bit bigger than a bumblebee, her short hooks of feet gripping tight, her long probe at an arrogant angle, her pulsing throat, brilliant green when her head turns left, crimson when it swivels right, she was sounding her whisper-like

Far from the glitz of Los Angeles, May hauled ashes from her cabin's stove at Dorland Mountain Colony in Temecula, California, during the winter of 1980.

signal as she sucked gnats out of their gossamer twirls in slanting sunlight. Now, from the top of an upright post at one corner of the deck of our shack and cabin, we've hung a slender cruet of red glass and filled it with sugar water which the Anna's can sip from a little cock at the base. Tiny helicopters, wings whirring that hold them poised in air, the hummingbirds are taking turns zooming in to feed right above our breakfast bowls, as we begin our first full day here in the high desert. . . .

For years, May had wanted to see the exotic birds, trees, and terrain of New Zealand. An invitation to a wedding there in December, 1987, gave her an immediate reason to go: Kathrine Switzer, Zan's friend from the sports world, was marrying Roger Robinson. "K" Switzer had been the first woman to register for and run the Boston Marathon so it was not surprising that the guests were world-class runners. May read her poem "Four-Word Lines" as part of the ceremony. It was followed by a

May holds a broadside of her poem "Four-Word Lines," a gift to the bride and groom (right) on the third terrace overlooking Wellington Harbor.

May (right), Roger Robinson, and Zan in front of Katherine Mansfield's family home in Wellington, New Zealand.

twelve-hour party, beginning May's active social life in Wellington. She was so busy during her two months there meeting New Zealand's artists and writers (all but her favorite, the reclusive novelist Janet Frame) that she hadn't the solitude for her own work. The many notes she took on a trip to South Island remained unused:

> We stopped the car high on a scenic outlook over the Pacific where tremendous waves hurled themselves at rough rock outcrops along the steep beach below. . . . And then we saw playing in a deep green vortex formed by the surrounding turbulent waters a pair of seals gold and black flashing in sunset light. They were huge, lazily tossing their sleek bodies over and under each other. We could hear the far echo of their deep hoarse cries.

By living in a remote off-season beach town for a month each spring or autumn, May avoided phone calls, appointments, visits, parties, and other obligations that

May at 13 Addy Road, Bethany Beach, Delaware. The house, called "Unsubdued" because of the uncontrollable kudzu, is the scene of her poem "Angels at 'Unsubdued'."

increasingly intruded on her time. This house in Bethany Beach (owned by Zan and her sister and mother) became May's refuge. Her duties there were self assigned: recording the sixty species of birds at feeders and birdbaths outside her window and taking long walks in the pine forest to observe wilder species.

THE WILLETS

One stood still, looking stupid. The other,
beak open, streaming a thin sound,
held wings out, took sideways steps,
stamping the salt marsh. It looked threatening.
The other still stood wooden, a decoy.

He stamp-danced closer, his wings arose,
their hinges straightened,
from the wedge-wide beak the thin sound
streaming agony-high—
in fear she would't stand? She stood.

Her back to him pretended—
was it welcome, or only dazed
admission of their fate?
Lifting, he streamed a warning
from his beak, and lit

upon her, trod upon her
back, both careful feet.
The wings held off his weight.
His tail pressed down, slipped off. She
animated. And both went back to fishing.

Wherever May traveled she used much of each day for writing. Here she worked on a poem in Everglades National Park, winter, 1972.

Chapter 7

Home to Utah

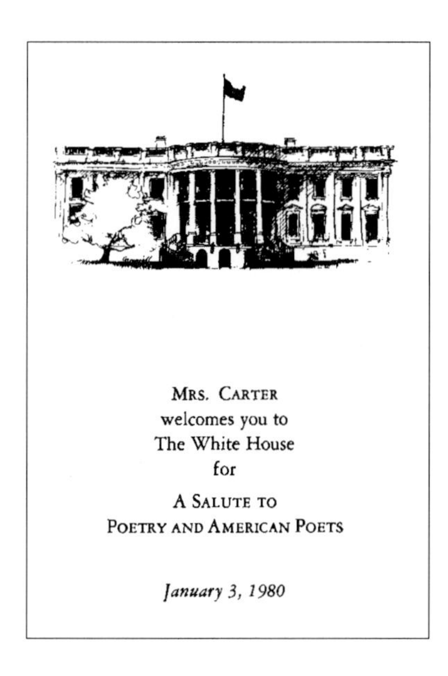
Mrs. Carter
welcomes you to
The White House
for
A Salute to
Poetry and American Poets

January 3, 1980

> *Welcome to a celebration of poetry and American poets. . . . Americans young and old, rich and poor, have found comfort, encouragement, joy, and challenge in American poetry. Our literary heritage is a proud one and an immortal part of our history. It is with great respect and admiration that I join this afternoon in paying tribute to America's poets.*

Thus wrote Roslyn Carter in the program for her gathering of poets at the White House, January 3, 1980. More than two hundred poets were there to shake hands

The New York Times/NYT Pictures

At the White House: Roslyn Carter with daughter, Amy, greeting Stanley Kunitz after the poetry reading. Others include, from right, John Ciardi, Jonathan Williams, behind him, and May Swenson.

with President and Mrs. Jimmy Carter. After going through the receiving line, the crowd strolled from room to room listening to poets reading: Louise Glück in the Red Room, Lucille Clifton in the Green Room, Richard Eberhart in the Blue Room, David Ignatow in the Diplomatic Reception Room, and more. Next day, May Swenson appeared on the front page of the *New York Times*.

"I didn't know the camera was aimed at me or I would have opened my right eye," May wrote to a friend who had sent her a telegram of congratulations. To editor John Nims, of the journal *Poetry*, she wrote "It actually was a thrill to shake hands with Jimmy Carter. I'm for him, and have been all along."

Another honor for May was writing and delivering the Phi Beta Kappa poem at Harvard University's commencement in 1982. To a friend she wrote:

> [John Kenneth] Galbraith and I made a funny couple marching beside each other in the procession across Harvard Yard and into the theatre—he about seven feet tall and I short, windblown, squinting into the sun. On stage we sat in tall carved chairs.

Listen, there's just one "Don't," one "Keep Off,"
one "Keep Away From"—and I don't mean "the Grass."
It is: *Don't be a clone*. . . .
It's good to be down there, level with nature,
like a plant, like an animal. Thoreau and
Whitman knew it. . . .
Like Billy Budd, stay sweet: The arm that flogs you
will fall off. . . .
. . . Get up, get out on the fresh edge
of things, away from the wow and flutter. Stand alone.
Take a breath of your own. Choose the wide-angle
view. That's something, maybe, you can begin to
learn to do, once you're *out* of college.

from May's Phi Beta Kappa poem,
"Some Quadrangles"

An earlier Ivy League honor, Yale's Bollingen Prize for poetry, came to May in 1981. In choosing May, the committee of three poets cited the "clarity of her vision and her delight in describing the pursuit of happiness in its unexampled forms." Previous winners had been Wallace Stevens, Marianne Moore, and Robert Frost, among others.

The chancellors and fellows of the Academy of American Poets were in Washington D.C., at the Library of Congress for the Academy's fiftieth anniversary in 1984. Front row seated: Robert Fitzgerald, Howard Nemorov, Marie Bullock, Stanley Kunitz, William Meredith, and Robert Penn Warren. Back row standing: W.S. Merwin, John Hollander, James Merrill, Mark Strand, May Swenson, David Wagoner, Daniel Hoffman, Anthony Hecht, and Mona Van Duyn.

Chancellor of the Academy of American Poets—May Swenson! With this title came responsibilities: more readings to give, poetry contests to judge, and tributes to deliver at memorial services sponsored by the Academy. A sad duty of May's was reading at the 1987 memorial tribute for Marie Bullock, who founded the Academy and nourished it for more than fifty years with her own money, energy, and love. May cherished her cordial friendship with Marie.

May on her way to receiving an honorary doctorate from Utah State University, June, 1987.

President Stanford Cazier confers the degree.

May returned to Utah in 1987 to receive an honorary doctorate from Utah State University. During her stay in Logan, May made a confession to her old college friend Edith Welch Morgan, who interviewed May for a 1987 article in the Logan *Herald Journal*.

"I have spent my life having fun," May said. "To make poetry is pleasure. When you write a poem it has surprises in it. It tells you things you never knew and there is no obligation in it. I don't feel I have to follow certain rules or write a certain way. Poetry lets you lead a very selfish life. I have not built my career by the usual academic route and have not sought a master's or doctorate degree nor accepted offers of a tenured position, and so it was with special surprise and pleasure that I learned of my university's intention to confer an honorary degree upon me."

Her brother Paul has written of this occasion:

> It was one of the last times we were all together. For May it had been an eventful few days. She had received word while in Logan that she'd been

May's family in Utah presented her with another diploma to signify her graduation "Summa Cum Whoopee."

May's eleventh book of poems, In Other Words, *was published in the fall of 1987. To promote sales and to be again with her family in Utah, she agreed to read at the Writers at Work Conference in Park City the next summer. She also read and signed books at the King's English Bookstore in Salt Lake City.*

awarded a MacArthur Fellowship. Sometime during that stay, in an on-campus hotel, she had written the astonishing poem, "My Name Was Called," which brought her childhood and her aging adulthood into collision.

After the food and the picture-taking, as the sun drained in my brother Dan's garden, we circled a bonfire. By flashlight May read her poems. I particularly remember her reading of a favorite of mine, "Two-Part Pear Able," the play of the flames on her face. She was within two-and-one-half years of her death.

May's MacArthur Fellowhip was for $380,000. From her first installment, she gave each of her brothers and sisters a $3,000 "Swenson Fellowship." Nieces and nephews received smaller fellowships.

May's final Swenson reunion was in spring, 1989, on her way back to Sea Cliff from the University of Washington in Seattle. There she had given the Theodore Roethke reading. Roethke was one of May's favorite poets, and she had felt honored to read in his name. In Utah, she felt tired from the asthma attacks she'd had during her trip, but she wanted to go through with her plans for a family dinner. "I want to

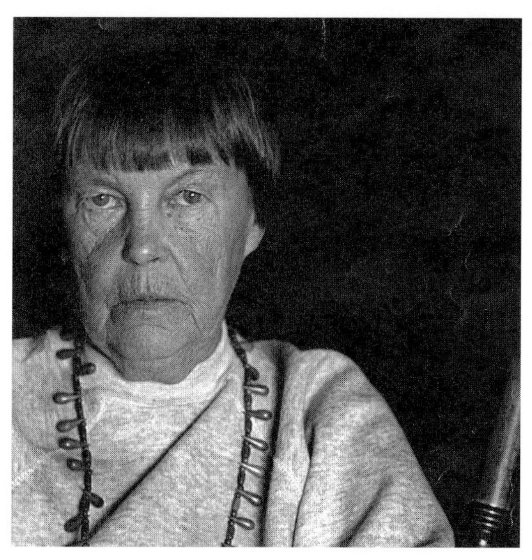

May was photographed by some of the best-known photographers of writers, among them Rollie McKenna, Tom Victor, Layle Silbert, and Annie Leibovitz. Yet May preferred the work of unknowns who at readings would snap her picture and mail it to her as a memory of the occasion. One such is this close-up by Mariana Cook, taken in 1984.

For a Life *magazine essay on contemporary poets, Annie Leibovitz came to Sea Cliff for a photo shoot. She prowled the first-floor rooms of the Kestrel's Nest, then upstairs through the bedrooms until her eyes fell on May's bed with its leopard-print sheets. Leibovitz immediately used them for her setting—and she had never read even one of May's fifteen cat poems. (See cover photo.) Long ago, May had written:*

Oh, to be a tigress,
and wear the same costume
summer, winter, autumn, spring;
to slink into a room,
and hear the women all exclaim:
"How chic you look, my dear!"
Oh, not to have to give a darn
what's being worn this year! . . .

May reads requests from her brothers, sisters, nieces, and nephews at a picnic in her brother Dan's backyard in Logan.

spend a lot of money," May told Margaret as they chose the restaurant and the menu. Margaret has written:

> The dinner was wonderful—expensive—in a private dining room of a French restaurant. I don't know if May had a premonition that it would be her last gathering with her family. We sang "Happy Seventy-Sixth Birthday, Dear May." She gave us each a copy of a new poem she had written for us, "Night Visits with the Family II."

This is the "large house" in May's poem "Last Day."

LAST DAY

I'm having a sunbath on the rug
alone in a large house facing south.
A tall window admits a golden trough
the length of a coffin in which I lie
in December, the last day of the year.
Sky in the window perfectly empty.
Naked tree limbs without wind.
No sounds reach my ears except their
ringing, and heart's thud hollow and
slow. Uncomplicated peace. Scarcely
a motion. Except a shadow that un-
detected creeps. On the table a clay pot,
a clump of narcissus lengthens its stems.
Blue buds sip the sun. Works of the clock
circle their ratchets. There is nothing
to wish for. Nothing to will.
What if this day is endless? No *new
year* to follow. Alteration done with.
A golden moment frozen, clenched.

Zan built the "large house" in Ocean View, Delaware, for use during winters. The furnace was a welcome change from the electric space heaters in Sea Cliff.

May's chess partner Sallie Reynolds from Sea Cliff spent the first weekend of December, 1989, with May and Zan in Delaware. Sallie writes:

> Saturday we drove to the breakwater at Ocean City to look for the purple sandpiper. May was tired. That night she had an asthma attack—the terrible kind that left her coughing and gasping till her whole body shook in spasms. Sunday morning she looked small and exhausted. After breakfast, she handed me a page from her working folder. The poem enchanted me, building into a whole with May's magic ties almost invisible yet strong enough to rescue the drowning:

"Celestial objects/ the farthest are the earliest/ the oldest the brightest"

May had turned her back to me at her desk. She said "Bodies don't last forever, you know. I think mine is wearing out. I may not live much longer."

I heard myself protesting. I'm not sure she said "Goodbye" when, a moment later, I left to catch my bus back to Sea Cliff. But she'd already said everything.

May died early the next morning from a heart attack brought on by high blood pressure and severe asthma.

FUNERAL SERVICES FOR

Anna Thilda May Swenson

Daughter of Dan A. & Margaret H. Swenson

Born May 28, 1913, Logan, Utah
Died December 4, 1989, Ocean View, Delaware

Services Saturday, December 9, 1989 at 12:00 Noon

Logan 18th Ward Chapel

President Glenn T. Baird Conducting

Dedication of the grave ...... Dan H. Swenson (brother)
Logan City Cemetery

PALLBEARERS — NEPHEWS

Swen Swenson, Steven Swenson, Curtis Swenson, Kevan Eyre, Rawlin Eyre, Dan Hall

HONORARY PALLBEARERS — NEPHEWS & NIECE

Don Swenson, Dan Swenson, Nikolai Turetsky, Jonathan Swenson, Robert Hall, Jordan Woodbury, Caitlin Swenson

Services

Family Prayer .... Roy Swenson (brother)

Piano Prelude .... Lorraine Self (cousin)
Medley of May's favorite hymns

Invocation .... George Swenson (brother)

Biographical Sketch .... Roy Swenson

Vocal Duet...... Beth Hall (sister) & Patty Tanner (niece)
"Look up to Him"

Memories .... Ruth Eyre & Grace Turetsky (sisters)

Vocal Solo .... Grace Turetsky (sister)
"I Will Lie down in Autumn"
(A poem by May Swenson,
set to music by Howard Swanson)

Selected Poems
by May Swenson .... Paul & Sharon Swenson (brother & sister-in-law)
Margaret Woodbury (sister)
Rozanne Knudson (friend)

Congregational Song .... Congregation
"The Spirit of God" (1st verse)

Speaker .... Lael Woodbury (brother-in-law)

Congregational Song .... Congregation
"True to the Faith" (1st Verse)

Benediction .... Sharon Swenson

Postlude .... Lorraine Self

The program from May's funeral. The family was careful to sing May's favorite Mormon hymns. Roy's talk included words May had once said to him:

Life is a mystery. We must not give ourselves airs. We are not the apex of creation. It is all evolving. We don't know what the answers will be.

May was buried in Logan City Cemetery. Carved on the pedestal of the granite bench on her grave are lines from her poem, "I Look at My Hand." On the bench's seat, here covered with snow, is carved her short poem "The Exchange." (See p. 162 for May's first draft of "The Exchange.")

THE ACADEMY OF AMERICAN POETS

A MEMORIAL TRIBUTE TO

MAY SWENSON

May Swenson

Thursday, March 28, 1991

The New-York Historical Society

7:00 p.m.

The Academy of American Poets sponsored a tribute reading for May, attended by her friends and fans in New York and by her sisters and brothers, who had traveled together from Utah.

Tribute readers were May's sister Margaret and eleven poets whose work May admired. May's college friend Veneta Nielsen made the long trip from Logan to read May's first published poem, "Three Hues of Melody."

Readers, left to right: Peter Davison, Alicia Ostriker, Irving Feldman, Veneta Nielsen, Margaret Swenson, Edward Field, Jane Mayhall, Mary Oliver, Judith Baumel, Daniel Hoffman, Diane Ackerman, and John Hollander.

Chapter 8

Afterwords / Afterphotos

May and Zan.

I like this photo of May and Zan; May, with her binoculars at the ready could be exclaiming over a bird she had just seen, or she could be giving Zan the word. Zan's eyes are amused; May's a mystery behind dark lenses. A photo to solve.

I met May Swenson some twenty-five years ago in the bar of the Waldorf Astoria. New York was gripped by mid-summer heat, and my college friend of ancient days, Rozanne Knudson, who had arranged the meeting, opted for the dark coolness of the hotel bar, assuring us that it had the best peanuts in town.

I remember being electrified when I first heard May read at a workshop at Westminster College in Salt Lake City, and again in 1977, at the University of Utah. We traveled to Utah State University in Logan to hear her read "Some Quadrangles," a section of which is about her school days there. And I was present at the Writers at Work Conference in Park City in 1988

May in Salt Lake City in the summer of 1972 with Paige and baby Eyre, two of the Bigelow children.

when she stole the show. After the program, she invited me to her hotel room and we talked into the night about Zan, who had not been able to make the trip; about my husband Richard, who was Zan's doctor and friend; what my kids were doing; and what I was writing. May seldom said much about herself.

I remember times she came to dinner and played with our children—how kind she was to them, pointing out to Richard and me all those things parents like to hear. I remember her intense interest in all around her. I felt I knew her not only because of a few uncomplicated conversations and visits, and our mutual love for Zan, but through her poems, which brought new life to me. I thank her for that, and I owe her.

Suzzanne Bigelow
Salt Lake City, June 1996

A fitting end for this collection of photos is May's drawing for Self-Portrait: Book People Picture Themselves *(Random House, 1976). Always a shy, private person, May reveals nothing of herself here.*

But in the poems to follow, readers will discover her heart and mind.

R.R. Knudson
Sea Cliff, New York, June 1996

May Swenson

ANTHOLOGY

A Life in Poems

THE TRUTH IS FORCED

Not able to be honest in person
I wish to be honest in poetry.
Speaking to you, eye to eye, I lie
because I cannot bear
to be conspicuous with the truth.
Saying it—all of it—would be
taking off my clothes.
I would forfeit my most precious properties:
distance, secrecy, privacy.
I would be exposed. And I would be
possessed. It would be an entire
surrender (to you, eye to eye).
You would examine me too closely.
You would handle me.
All your eyes would swarm me.
I'd be forever after hotly dressed
in your cloying, itching, greedy bees.
Whether you are one or two or many
it is the same. Really, I feel as if
one pair of eyes were a whole hive.
So I lie (eye to eye)
by leaving the core of things unvoiced
or else by offering a dummy
in place of myself.

One must be honest somewhere. I wish
to be honest in poetry.
With the written word.
Where I can say and cross out
and say over and say around
and say on top of and say in between
and say in symbol, in riddle,
in double meaning, under masks
of any feature, in the skins
of every creature.
And in my own skin, naked.
I am glad, indeed I dearly crave
to become naked in poetry,
to force the truth
through a poem,
which, when it is made, if real,
not a dummy, tells me
and then you (all or any, eye to eye)
my whole self,
the truth.

THE POPLAR'S SHADOW

When I was little, when
the poplar was in leaf,
its shadow made a sheaf,
the quill of a great pen
dark upon the lawn
where I used to play.

Grown, and long away
into the city gone,
I see the pigeons print
a loop in air and, all
their wings reversing, fall
with silver undertint
like poplar leaves, their seams
in the wind blown.

Time's other side, shown
as a flipped coin, gleams
on city ground
when I see a pigeon's feather:
little and large together,
the poplar's shadow is found.

Staring at here,
and superposing then,
I wait for when.
What shapes will appear?
Will great birds swing
over me like gongs?
The poplar plume belongs
to what enormous wing?

WORKING ON WALL STREET

What's left of the sunset's watered blood
settles between the slabs of Wall Street.
Winter rubs the sky bruise-blue as flesh.
We head down into the subway, glad
the cars are padded with bodies so we
keep warm. Emptied from tall closets
where we work, on the days' shelves
reached by elevators, the heap of us,
pressed by iron sides, dives forward under
the city—parcels shipped out in a trunk.

The train climbs from its cut to the trestle.
Sunset's gone. Those slabs across the murky
river have shrunk to figurines, reflecting
the blush of neon—a dainty tableau, all
pink, on the dresser-top of Manhattan—
eclipsed as we sink into the tunnel.
The train drops and flattens for the long
bore under Brooklyn.

Night, a hiatus hardly real, tomorrow
this double rut of steel will racket us back
to the city. We, packages in the trade
made day after day, will tumble out of
hatches on the Street, to be met by swags
of wind that scupper off those roofs
(their upper windows blood-filled by the sun).
Delivered into lobbies, clapped into upgoing
cages, sorted to our compartments, we'll be
stamped once more for our wages.

HORSES IN CENTRAL PARK

Colors of horses like leaves or stones
or wealthy textures
liquors of light

The skin of a plum that's more than ripe
sheathes a robust
cloven rump

Frosty plush of lilies
for another's head
ears and nostrils funneled are their cones

Of sere October leaves
this gaunt roan's hide
freckled dun and red

Here's a mole-gray back
and darker dappled haunch
tail and forelock mauve like smoke

This coal-colored stallion
flake of white on his brow
is slippery silk in the sun

Fox-red bay
and buckskin blond as wheat
Burgundy mare with tasseled mane of jet

Sober chestnut burnished
by his sweat
to veined and glowing oak

Seal-brown mustang
with stocking-feet
Pinto in patched and hooded domino

Naked palomino
is smooth peeled willow
or marble under water or clean morning snow

AT EAST RIVER

Tugboat: A large shoe
shuffles the floor of water,
leaving a bright scrape.

Floating Gulls: Ballet slippers, dirty-white,
walk awkward backward.
Bobbing closer: yellow-pointed painted
wooden shoes.

The Bay: Flat, shiny, rustling
like parquet under the bridge's
balustrade of gray garlands.

On the Bridge: Slow skates of cars (a distant whisper)
and the long swishing foot of a train.

A Plane: Turns on its elegant heel:
a spark, a click
of steel on blue.

That Steamer: The top of a short boot, red and black,
budging deep water wading to the sea.

Brooklyn: A shelf of old shoes,
needing repair,
but clean knots of smoke
are being tied and untied.

FOUR-WORD LINES

Your eyes are just
like bees, and I
feel like a flower.
Their brown power makes
a breeze go over
my skin. When your
lashes ride down and
rise like brown bees'
legs, your pronged gaze
makes my eyes gauze.
I wish we were
in some shade and
no swarm of other
eyes to know that
I'm a flower breathing
bare, laid open to
your bees' warm stare.
I'd let you wade
in me and seize
with your eager brown
bees' power a sweet
glistening at my core.

WHILE SEATED IN A PLANE

On a kicked-up floor of cloud
a couch of cloud, deformed and fluffy;
far out, more celestial furniture—fat chairs

slowly puffing forth their airy stuffing.
On dream-feet I walked into that large
parlor on cool pearl—but found it far

between the restless resting places.
Pinnacles, detaching, floating from their bases,
swelled to turbulent beds and tables,

ebbed to ebullient chairs,
then footstools that, degraded,
flowed with the floor before I could get there.

One must be a cloud to occupy a house of cloud.
I twirled in my dream, and was deformed
and reformed, making many faces,

refusing the fixture of a solid soul.
So came to a couch I could believe,
although it altered

its facile carvings, at each heave
became another throne.
Neither dissolved nor solid, I was settled

and unsettled in my placeless chair.
A voluntary mobile, manybodied, I traded
shape for the versatility of air.

THE TALL FIGURES OF GIACOMETTI

We move by means of our mud bumps.
We bubble as do the dead but more slowly.

The products of excruciating purges
we are squeezed out thin hard and dry.

If we exude a stench it is petrified sainthood.
Our feet are large crude fused together

solid like anvils. Ugly as truth is ugly
we are meant to stand upright a long time

and shudder without motion
under the scintillating pins of light

that dart between our bodies
of pimpled mud and your eyes.

AUGUST 19, PAD 19

. . . . 8 days without weighing anything.
Not knowing up from down.
Positioned for either breech birth
or urn burial. My mission the practice
of catching up by slowing down,
I am the culmination of a 10-storey bottle,
in 3 disconnectable parts,
being fueled with seething vapor
becoming water becoming fire.
I am the throbbing cork about to pop.

. . . . About to be dragged backward
through 121 sunsets,
not to bathe or drink bare light raw air.
My $75 pencil in my grotesque hand
prepares to float above the clipboard
strapped to my right knee.

. . . . T minus 10 and counting.
Over my obsolete epiderm redundant with
hairs and pits of moisture
I wear my new, rich, inflatable skin,
the bicep patch a proud tattoo,
a galaxy of 50 States,
my telemetric skull, a glossy cupola
resembling the glans of an Aztec god.
My sliding jaw, my safe transparent face
closes. Lungs, you will learn
to breathe hydrogen.

. . . . T minus 10 and counting.
Belted and bolted in, the capsule plugged,
when my 2 umbilical hoses tear free,
I shall increase to the bulk of 7 men,
be halfway to Africa in 12 minutes,
40 seconds. A bead beyond the bulge of earth,
extruded, banished. Till hooked to
the swivel of my ellipse,
I'm played through day and night and east
and west, reeled between apogee and perigee.

. . . . The erector stiffly swoons to its
concrete grave.

. . . . T minus 10 and holding.
Below in the blockhouse, pressed to the
neck of flame, a thumb on the piston
pulses LIFT OFF or ABORT.
My teleological aim the ovary moon,
will I ignite, jump, inject into the sky today
my sparkle of steel sperm?

. . . . Never so helpless, so choked with power.
Never so impotent, so important.
So naked, wrapped, equipped, and immobile,

cared for by 5000 nurses.
Let them siphon my urine to the nearest star.
Let it flare and spin like a Catherine.

. . . . T minus 10 . . . . The click of countdown stops.
My pram and mummycase, this trap's
tumescent tube's still locked to wet,
magnetic, unpredictable earth.
All my systems go, but oh,
an anger of the air won't let me go.
On the screen the blip is MISSION SCRUBBED.

. . . . Be dry my eye for nothing must leak
in here. If a tear forms, instruct the duct
to suck it back. Float, tadpole heart,
behind your slats of bone.
Keep your vibration steady, my switch of blood.
Eyeball in your nook of crepe
behind the ice shield of my window-face,
and ear within your muff of radio,
count taps against the hatch's darkening pane.
Out on the dome some innocent drops of rain.
A puny jolt of thunder. Lightning's golden sneer.

Note: On August 19, 1965, the launch of Gemini 5 from Pad 19 at Cape Canaveral was "scrubbed" because of weather.

THE JAMES BOND MOVIE

The popcorn is greasy,
and I forgot to bring a
Kleenex. A pill that's a
bomb inside the stomach
of a man inside The
Embassy blows up. Eruc-
tations of flame, luxur-
ious cauliflowers, gigan-
ticize into motion. The
entire 29-ft. screen is
orange, is crackling
flesh and brick bursting,
blackening, smithereened.
I unwrap a Dentyne and,
while jouncing my teeth
in rubber-tongue-smart-
ing clove, try with the
2-inch-wide paper to
blot butter off my fingers. A bubble-
bath, room-sized, in which 14 girls,
delectable and sexless, are twist-
topped Creamy Freezes (their
blond, red, brown, pinkish, lav-
endar or silver wiglets screw-
ed that high, and varnished),
scrub-tickle a lone male,
whose chest has just the
right amount and distri-
bution of not too curly
hair. He's nervously
pretending to defend
his modesty. His
crotch, below the
waterline, is
also below the
frame—but unsubmerged
all 28 slick foamy boobs.
Their makeup fails to let
the girls look naked.
Caterpillar lashes, black
and thick, lush lips
glossed pink like the gum
I pop and chew, Contacts
on all the eyes that are
mostly blue, they're
nose-perfect replicas of
each other. I've got
most of the grease off and
on to this little square
of paper. I'm folding it
now, making creases with
my nails.

FACE TO FACE

In February life stood still.
Birds unwilling to fly, and I
chafed at the landscape like a boat
that rubs the jetty it's tied to.

Trees stood with backs turned all one way.
Snow depth was measured by dead straws.
Footprints aged out there on the crust.
Under the pall even language faded.

One day something came up to the window.
Work stopped. I looked up.
Colors burned. Everything turned around.
The ground and I sprang at each other.

—Tomas Tranströmer
(translated from the Swedish by May Swenson)

ON THE ROAD

The full day is never the great day.
The best day is the day of thirst.

Yes there is goal and purpose to our effort
but the road, the road is our journey's worth.

The best meal is a nightlong rest;
over a little fire, bread broken in haste.

The place slept in only once
is the safest place, with dreams of song.

Break camp, break camp! The big day dawns.
Boundless is our adventure.

—Karin Boye
(translated from the Swedish by May Swenson)

WATCHING THE JETS LOSE TO BUFFALO AT SHEA

The feel of that leather baby
solid against your sternum,
you hug its skull and bottom
between huge huddled shoulders.
It's wrapped in your arms and wedged
under the hard muzzle
of your stuck-out faceguard.

Your thighs pumping, you run
to deliver the baby
to a cradle of grass at the goalposts.
But it's bumped from your arms,
and you're mounted
as if your back were leather.
Your legs cut away, you fold,

you tumble like a treetrunk.
Your brain's for the ground to split
like a leather egg, but it doesn't.
Your helmet takes the concussion.
Sent aloft by a leather toe,
a rugged leather baby
dropped from the sky and slammed

into the sling of your arms.
Oh, the feel of that leather bundle.
Oh, what a blooper and fumbler
you are, that you couldn't nest it,
that you lost and couldn't nurse it,
long enough to lay it
in a cradle of grass at the goalposts.

WOMEN

Women
should be
pedestals
moving
pedestals
moving
to the
motions
of men

Or they
should be
little horses
those wooden
sweet
oldfashioned
painted
rocking
horses

the gladdest things in the toyroom

The
pegs
of their
ears
so familiar
and dear
to the trusting
fists
To be chafed

feelingly
and then
unfeelingly
To be
joyfully
ridden
rockingly
ridden until
the restored

egos dismount and the legs stride away

Immobile
sweetlipped
sturdy
and smiling
women
should always
be waiting

willing
to be set
into motion
Women
should be
pedestals
to men

PRISON ARCHITECTURE

Medieval, even noble, the domain looks from the air,
and in the shifting frame in front of my easy chair:
the guard tower like a king's, within the wall

of the decahedron a benign empire's sprawl.
Enlargement as the lens descends: at massive clanging
gates, the knights—black mostly, some white—are shown

at wassail, it seems, misshapen tankards banging
allegiance to the electric throne.
Vaulted corridors shake with awesome uproar, fanatic

faces bulge, all teeth and eyes. Pull-back is automatic:
the focus narrows, rises to a—stronghold, if you will,
but trim—castle keep in the foliage of a hill.

UNDER THE BABY BLANKET

Under the baby blanket 47 years old you are
asleep on the worn too-short Leatherette sofa.

Along with a watermelon and some peaches from
the beach cottage, you brought home this gift

from your Mom. "Just throw it in the van," you
said you said, "I haven't time to talk about it."

She had wanted to tell how she handstitched and
appliquéd the panels—a dozen of them—waiting

for you to be born: 12 identical sunbonneted
little girls, one in each square, in different

colors of dresses doing six different things.
And every tiny stitch put in with needle and

thimble. "It had to take months, looks like,"
I said. "Well, Mom's Relief Society ladies

must have helped," you said. One little girl
is sweeping, one raking, another watering a plant

in a pot, one dangling a doll dressed exactly
like herself. One is opening a blue umbrella.

At center is a little girl holding a book, with
your initial on the cover! I was astonished:

"A Matriarchal Blessing, predicting your future!"
(But, wait a minute, I thought. How did she know

you wouldn't be a boy? Was she also sewing
another blanket, with little boys in its squares:

holding hammer, riding tricycle, playing with
dog, batting ball, sailing boat, and so on?)

I asked for the baby blanket—which *is* a work
of art—to be hung on the wall above the sofa

where I could study it. You refused. You
lay down under it, bare legs drawn up, a smudge

of creosote on one knee. Almost covered with
little girls 47 years old you've gone to sleep.

SLEEPING WITH BOA

I show her how to put her arms around me,
but she's much too small.
What's worse, she doesn't understand.
And,
although she lies beside me, sticking
out her tongue, it's herself she licks.

She likes my stroking hand.
And,
even lets me kiss.
But, at my demand:
"Now, do it to me, like this,"
she backs off with a hiss.

What's in her little mind?
Jumping off the bed,
she shows me her behind,
but curls up on the rug instead.
I beg her to return. At first, she did,
then went and hid

under the covers. She's playing with my feet!
"Oh, Boa, come back. Be sweet.
Lie against me here where I'm nice and warm.
Settle down. Don't claw, don't bite.
Stay with me tonight."
Seeming to consent, she gives a little whine.

Her deep, deep pupils meet mine
with a look that holds a flood . . .
but not my brand.
Not at all.
And,
what's worse, she's much too small.

A RESCUE

In the middle of the line
under my reading eye
a spot of fog. It makes
faint an *e*, then a *y*,
and travels to the right.
In the next line the spot
expands, shifts and erases
a whole word. I close my
eyes and see a tiny bright
buzz saw that flickers.
Opened, my eye finds it
still there, in the air,
enlarged. I swallow a
pill, hoping to halt the
pain before it begins.
Eyes have roots in the
brain. In their transparent
prisms where blossoms of
image spring, the smallest
blight could shrink the
scope of consciousness
forever. I go to the mirror.
One eye sees itself, but
the other half of my face
is fog, except for a
quivering, toothy moon
there, which transforms
to a spiral. This is
dizzying. I darken the
room, I go to bed, I pull
the sheet over my head.
I will think only of sinking
slowly into soft layers of
cloud. I want to descend
all the way down to brain's
end and, without weight or
feature, slip under the skin
of sleep.

Episodes in the past, I
remember comet-like, came
with other unpredictable signs
and symptoms. Tongue went
numb, ears went deaf, I
clutched my hair where half
my skull throbbed like a
fisted drum, while flakes
of light changed pattern
behind one eyelid. When
the pain in eye socket, nape
and skull bone began, it grew
so cruel I moaned and rolled
in the bed for hours.
I had at last to vomit.
Only then, cold water splashed
over face and temples, head
in a cold cloth tightly bound,
I'd crawl back into bed,

entirely spent, and sleep
the day away. When rid of
it, sometimes by twilight,
limp but clear-eyed, hungry,
I'd go downstairs. Absence
of pain was a rescue.
Precious, delicious were
ordinary things: a bite of
bread, swallow of coffee,
sight of a streak of late
sun on the kitchen floor.
I could barely lift a hand,
yet relief brought a rush
of ecstasy. Sight sharp,
spine straight, I filled up
with joy and power. Almost
worth the hideous pain,
the sweet reward of its
riddance.

No pain this time. Today
only its dreaded expectation.
In a quarter hour the drug
begins to control the rate
of capillary flow in neck
and head, narrowing the
cranial pathways of blood
going to my brain. I can
relax in a gradual float
toward sleep, entertained
by the array of geometric
phantoms performing within
the focus space before (or
is it behind?) my left eye:
A tiny spectral triangle
revolves and slyly turns
tetrahedral. Outline of
a luminous cube replaces a
hazy cross. That fades
when twin pyramids, set base
to base, glide forward,
their angles disjoining into
loops that tie into a knot.
It glints and spins, but
finally simplifies to an
almost perfect figure eight,
which pulses, and slowly
pales, then sinks out of
"sight." The show already
over? I'm disappointed,
want to dive after it, to
where, deep in my brain,
surely other never-seen
brilliants teem. Somehow
I succeed. I'm in dream
dimension now. I can drag
back into "view" a final
sparkler. It organizes
instantly its golden points
and planes into a ziggurat.
Blissful symbol. I go on
sleeping.

THE PURE SUIT OF HAPPINESS

The pure suit of happiness,
not yet invented. How I long
to climb into its legs,

fit into its sleeves, and zip
it up, pull the hood
over my head. It's got

a face mask, too, and gloves
and boots attached. It's
made for me. It's blue. It's

not too heavy, not too
light. It's my right.
It has its own weather,

which is youth's breeze,
equilibrated by the ideal
thermostat of maturity,

and built in, to begin with,
fluoroscopic goggles of
age. I'd see through

everything, yet be happy.
I'd be suited for life. I'd
always look good to myself.

A WISH

Out of an hour I built a hut
and like a Hindu sat
immune in the wind of time

From a hair I made a path
and walked and both
rock and wilderness became

my space and thoroughfare
With sorrow for a skin
I felt no wound

Pleasant power like a nut
ripened and split within me
Where there had been wrath

it loosened all the world
to quiet noonday
My face in the rock my name

on the wildest tree
My flesh the heath
of a peaceful clime

THE LOWERING*

The flag is folded
lengthwise, and lengthwise again,
folding toward the open edge,
so that the union of stars on the blue
field remains outward in full view;
a triangular folding is then begun
at the striped end,
by bringing the corner of the folded edge
to the open edge;
the outer point, turned inward along the open edge,
forms the next triangular fold:
the folding continued so, until the end is reached,
the final corner tucked between
the folds of the blue union,
the form of the folded flag is found to resemble that
of a 3-cornered pouch, or thick cocked hat.

Take this flag, John Glenn, instead of a friend;
instead of a brother, Edward Kennedy, take this flag;
instead of a father, Joe Kennedy, take this flag;
this flag instead of a husband, Ethel Kennedy, take this flag;
this 9-times-folded red-white-striped, star-spotted-blue flag,
tucked and pocketed neatly,
Nation, instead of a leader, take this folded flag.
Robert Kennedy, coffin without coverlet,
beside this hole in the grass,
beside your brother, John Kennedy,
in the grass,
take, instead of a country,
this folded flag;
Robert Kennedy, take this
hole in the grass.

*Arlington Cemetery, June 8, 1968.

THE REST OF MY LIFE

Sleeping Alone

Waiting for first light,
for the lift of the curtain,
for the world to ripen,
tumbling toward the sun,

I lie on my side,
head sunk in the pillow,
legs upfolded,
as if for Indian burial.

My arms are friends
relaxed beside each other.
One hand, open, touches,
brings warmth to the other.

A Spring Morning

Your right hand and my left
hand, as if they were bodies
fitting together, face each other.

As if we were dancing. But
we are in bed. The thumb of your
hand touches my cheek. My head

feels the cool of the pillow.
Your profile, eye and ear and lip
asleep, has already gone

through the doorway of your dream.
The round-faced clock ticks on,
on the shelf in dawnlight.

Your hand has met mine,
but doesn't feel my cheek is wet.
From the top of the oak

outside the window, the oriole
over and over repeats its
phrase, a question.

Unable to Write It

Tears do not make good ink.
Their message invisible,
no one reads this hurt.

I lie alone in dirt despair.
Alone beside one who does not feel
lightning strike and agony crackle.

I sink into black, the inkwell
wordless, filled with tears.

What Matters

It may be that it doesn't matter
who or what or why you love.

(Maybe it matters when, and for how long.)
Of course, what matters is how strong.

Maybe the forbidden, the unbelievable,
or what doesn't respond—
what grabs all and gives nothing—
what is ghoul or ghost,
what proves you a fool,
shrinks you, shortens your life,
if you love it, *it* doesn't matter.
Only the love matters—
the stubbornness, or the helplessness.

At a certain chemical instant
in early youth, love's trigger is cocked.
Whatever moves into focus
behind the cross hairs, magnifies,
is marked for target, injected with
magic shot. But the target doesn't matter.

The Rest of My Life

I'm the one
who'll be with me
for the rest of my life.

I'm the one
who'll enjoy myself,
take care of myself,
be loveable, so as to love
myself for the rest
of my life.

Arms, be strong to hold me.
Eyes, be with me.
Will you be with me
for the rest of my life?

I'm the one,
the only one,
the one who won't leave me
for the rest of my life.

I'm One

I do not have.
I do not expect.
I do not owe.

I'm one,
the only one,
free in my life.

Each day perfect,
each day a thousand years.
Time is in me.

I swallow the sun.
I'm the one, the only
one in my life.

Oh, windless day
within me.
Oh, silence and sun.

STRIPPING AND PUTTING ON

I always felt like a bird blown through the world.
I never felt like a tree.

I never wanted a patch of this earth to stand in,
that would stick to me.

I wanted to move by whatever throb my muscles
sent to me.

I never cared for cars, that crawled on land or
air or sea.

If I rode, I'd rather another animal: horse, camel,
or shrewd donkey.

Never need a nest, unless for the night, or when
winter overtook me.

Never wanted an extra skin between mine and the sun,
for vanity or modesty.

Would rather not have parents, had no yen for a child,
and never felt brotherly.

But I'd borrow or lend love of friend. Let friend be
not stronger or weaker than me.

Never hankered for Heaven, or shied from a Hell,
or played with the puppets Devil and Deity.

I never felt proud as one of the crowd under
the flag of a country.

Or felt that my genes were worth more or less than beans,
by accident of ancestry.

Never wished to buy or sell. I would just as well
not touch money.

Never wanted to own a thing that I wasn't born with.
Or to act by a fact not discovered by me.

I always felt like a bird blown through the world.
But I would like to lay

the egg of a world in a nest of calm beyond
this world's storm and decay.

I would like to own such wings as light speeds on,
far from this globule of night and day.

I would like to be able to put on, like clothes,
the bodies of all those

creatures and things hatched under the wings
of that world.

THE EXCHANGE (FIRST DRAFT)

Now my body flat – the ground
breathes. I'll be the grass,
too rich & populous ~~the~~ to mind
Earth take thought my mouth be moss
moss be my mouth
a disk
field go walking with searing
pierce down
will peer on you my ~~curious~~ eye

for am my mouth is moss
when I be moss lean
lean
I will be time and steady to be
evening you would ~~earth~~ be clock
I will stand/a tree here
never to know another spot
wind be ~~my~~ motor bird ~~my~~ be pawn
invite me to
water sing to me from your bed

Index of Dates

May Swenson kept a master index in which she noted publication information as well as the date and place she began each of her poems. Those dates follow the poems listed here.

At East River (March 1957)
August 19, Pad 19 (August 19, 1965)
Creation (1932)
The Desk. The Body (October 2, 1979)
Electronic Sound (July 17, 1966)
The Exchange (August 6, 1961)
Feel Me (March 4, 1964)
Four-Word Lines (August 24, 1963)
Horses in Central Park (1954)
How Everything Happens (October 1960)
I Look at My Hand (March 12, 1961)
Italian Sampler (October, 1960)
The James Bond Movie (June 26, 1967)
July 4th (July 6, 1972)
Last Day (December 31, 1986)
The Lowering (June 8, 1968)
My Mother and Father Came to See (1954)
Oh, to Be a Tigress (Pre-1950)
The Poplar's Shadow (1954)
The Pregnant Dream (June 7, 1965)
Prison Architecture (September 10, 1971)
The Pure Suit of Happiness (April 6, 1971)

Rainbow Hummingbird Lamplight (Winter 1980)
A Rescue (January 2, 1989)
Riding the "A" (May 15, 1959)
The Rest of My Life (November 1, 1978)
Sleeping with Boa (November 28, 1980)
Snow in New York (February 19, 1958)
Some Quadrangles (January 1982)
Something Goes By (March 1956)
Stripping and Putting On (September 7, 1963)
The Tall Figures of Giacometti (August 24, 1965)
The Truth Is Forced (March 16, 1961)
Under the Baby Blanket (June 30, 1979)
Watching the Jets Lose to Buffalo at Shea (1975)
While Seated in a Plane (May 29, 1963)
The Willets (May 10, 1970)
A Wish (January 1953)
Women (July 20, 1967)
Working on Wall Street (March 1956)

Books by May Swenson

Another Animal (1954)
A Cage of Spines (1958)
To Mix with Time (1963)
Poems to Solve (1966)
Half Sun Half Sleep (1967)
Iconographs (1970)
More Poems to Solve (1971)
Windows & Stones (1972) (Translated from Tomas Tranströmer)
The Guess and Spell Coloring Book (1976)
New and Selected Things Taking Place (1978)
In Other Words (1987)
The Love Poems (1991)
The Complete Poems to Solve (1993)
Nature (1994)
May Out West (1996)

Awards Won by May Swenson

Introduction Prize of the Poetry Center of the New York City YM/YWCA (1953)
Rockefeller Writing Fellowship (1955)
William Rose Benet Poetry Prize of the Poetry Society of America (1958)
Longview Foundation Prize (1959)
John Simon Guggenheim Memorial Foundation Grant (1959)
Amy Lowell Traveling Scholarship (1960)
National Institute of Arts and Letters Grant (1960)
The Ford Foundation Grant for Poets and Writers Combined with Theatre Group (1964)
Utah State University Distinguished Service Gold Medal (1967)
Rockefeller Foundation Grant (1967)
Brandeis University Creative Arts Award (1967)
Shelley Memorial Award of the Poetry Society of America (1968)
Academy of American Poets Fellowship (1969)
American Institute of Graphic Arts 50 Books of the Year (for *Iconographs*) (1970)
International Poetry Forum Medal (1972)
National Endowments for the Arts Award (1974)
Bollingen Award (shared with Howard Nemerov) (1981)
The Golden Rose of the New England Poetry Club (1983)
Honorary Ph.D. in Literature, Utah State University (1987)
Utah State University's Centennial Award (1987)
MacArthur Foundation Fellowship (1987)
Literary Lion of the New York Public Library (1988)

This page constitutes an extension of the copyright page (iv). The following poems were previously published as indicated; our grateful acknowledgement to the publishers.

in *Half Sun Half Sleep*. Copyright © 1967 by May Swenson: "On the Road" by Karin Boye. Translated by May Swenson; "The Pregnant Dream."

in *Iconographs*. Copyright © 1970 by May Swenson: "The James Bond Movie" and "The Power House."

in *Windows & Stones*. Copyright © 1972 by May Swenson: "Face to Face" by Tomas Tranströmer. Translated by May Swenson.

in *New & Selected Things Taking Place*. Copyright © 1978 by May Swenson: "At East River," "August 19, Pad 19," "Horses in Central Park," "Italian Sampler," "July 4th," "The Lowering," "The Pure Suit of Happiness," "Riding the 'A'," "Snow in New York," "The Tall Figures of Giacometti," "Watching the Jets Lose to Buffalo at Shea," "While Seated in a Plane," "A Wish," "Women," and "Working on Wall Street."

in *In Other Words*. Copyright © 1987 by May Swenson. Reprinted by permission of Alfred A. Knopf, Inc. All rights reserved. "Under the Baby Blanket," eighteen lines from "Rainbow Hummingbird Lamplight," and thirteen lines from "Some Quadrangles."

in *The Love Poems of May Swenson*. Copyright © 1991 by The Literary Estate of May Swenson. Reprinted by permission of Houghton-Mifflin Co."Four-Word Lines."

in *The Complete Poems to Solve*. Copyright © 1993 The Literary Estate of May Swenson. Reprinted with the permission of Simon & Schuster Books for Young Readers. All rights reserved. "Electronic Sound" and "How Everything Happens."

in *The Wonderful Pen of May Swenson*. Copyright © 1993 by The Literary Estate of May Swenson. Reprinted with permission of the Estate. Eight lines from "Oh, To Be a Tigress."

in *Nature*. Copyright © 1994 by The Literary Estate of May Swenson. Reprinted with permission of Houghton-Mifflin Co. All rights reserved. "Feel Me," "I Look at My Hand," "Last Day," "The Poplar's Shadow," "Stripping and Putting On," "The Truth is Forced," and "The Willets."

in *May Out West*. Copyright © 1996 by The Literary Estate of May Swenson: twelve lines from "Something Goes By."